W9-ACI-394

ILLINOIS CENTRAL COLLEGE
PN6110.C5S3x
STACKS
Stardust & holly :

A12900 303537

PN
6110
.C5
S3x

SHIPMAN
Stardust & Holly

WITHDRAWN

Illinois Central College
Learning Resources Center

Stardust & Holly

Stardust & Holly

POEMS AND SONGS
OF CHRISTMAS

Selected by

DOROTHY MIDDLEBROOK SHIPMAN, comp.

❦

GRANGER BOOKS
MIAMI, FLORIDA

56487

I.C.C. LIBRARY

PN
6110
.C5
S3 X

FIRST PUBLISHED 1932
REPRINTED 1976

PRINTED IN THE UNITED STATES OF AMERICA

TO THE MEMORY OF
AUNT NELLIE,
DISPENSER OF CHRISTMAS SPIRIT
THE YEAR 'ROUND

Acknowledgments

THE editor desires to thank the following publishers for their kind permission to use the poems included in this volume:

D. APPLETON & Co. for "Yule-tide Fires," Anonymous; "Waiting for the Kings" by R. L. Gales; "The Waits" by M. Nightingale, copyright 1923.

RICHARD G. BADGER for "Babushka" by Edith M. Thomas.

THE CENTURY COMPANY for "Song of the Christmas Trees" by Blanche Elizabeth Wade; "Christmas Eve" by Mary Mapes Dodge; "The Little Gray Lamb" by Archibald Beresford Sullivan.

THOMAS Y. CROWELL COMPANY for "The Least of Carols" by Sophie Jewett.

DODD, MEAD AND COMPANY for "Christmas Eve" from *Fleet Street Eclogues* by John Davidson; "The Lamb, Child" from *The Poetry of Father Tabb* by John Banister Tabb.

E. P. DUTTON & Co. for "That Holy Thing" by George MacDonald; "Out of the Shadow" by Michael Fairless.

DOUBLEDAY DORAN COMPANY for "The Shepherds in Judea" by Mary Austin; "Gates and Doors, A Ballad of Christmas Eve" from *Main Street and Other Poems* by Joyce Kilmer; "Christmas Folk-song" from *Selected Poems* by Lizette Woodworth Reese.

H. W. GRAY for "Provençal Noël of Nicholas Saboly" and "Neighbors of Bethlehem" published with music by them.

HARCOURT, BRACE AND COMPANY for "A Country Carol," and "Holly Carol" from *Ballads and Lyrics*, copyright 1925, by Margaret Widdemer.

HARPER AND BROTHERS for "Litany of the Black People" from *Copper Sun* by Countee Cullen.

HENRY HOLT AND COMPANY for "A Ballad of Christmas" by Walter de la Mare.

HOUGHTON MIFFLIN COMPANY for "Kriss Kringle" by Thomas Bailey Aldrich; "The Lame Shepherd" and "The Kings of the East" by Katherine Lee Bates; "Tryste Noël" by Louise Imogen Guiney; "Christmas Bells" and "The Three Kings" by Henry Wadsworth Longfellow; "A Christmas Carol" by James Russell Lowell; "Song of a Shepherd Boy at Bethlehem" by Josephine Preston Peabody; "A Christmas Wish" by Celia Thaxter; "Shoe or Stocking" by Edith M. Thomas; "A Christmas Carmen" by John Greenleaf Whittier.

LITTLE, BROWN AND COMPANY for "The Little Christmas Tree" by Susan Coolidge.

ROBERT M. McBRIDE AND COMPANY for "Courtesy" by Hilaire Belloc.

THE MACMILLAN COMPANY for "Hora Christi" by Alice Brown; "How Far Is It to Bethlehem" by Frances Chesterton; "The Oxen" from *Collected Poems of Thomas Hardy*; "Star of My Heart" by Vachel Lindsay; "Before the Paling of the Stars,"

Acknowledgments ix

"A Christmas Carol" and "The Shepherds Had an Angel" by Christina Rossetti; "A Christmas Carol" by Sara Teasdale from *Helen of Troy and Other Poems;* "A Toast" by Marguerite Wilkinson.

PUBLIC SCHOOL PUB. CO. for "Christmas Eve" from *Songs of Treetop and Meadow* by Marguerite Merington.

G. P. PUTNAM's SONS for "Wayside Music" by Charles Henry Crandall; "Attendants" by David Morton from *Ships in Harbor;* "The Shepherd Who Stayed" by Theodosia Garrison from *As the Larks Rise.*

CHARLES SCRIBNER's SONS for "A Christmas Hymn for Children" by Josephine Dodge Daskam; "Christmas Treasures," "Jest 'Fore Christmas" and "The Three Kings of Cologne" by Eugene Field.

SOUTH WEST PRESS for "I Do Not Like a Roof To-night" from *Flame in the Wind* by Grace Noll Crowell.

FREDERICK A. STOKES CO. for "Shall I to the Byre Go Down" and "Six Green Singers" from *Come Christmas* by Eleanor Farjeon, copyright 1927; and for "The Carol of the Fir Tree" from *Collected Poems* Vol. 2 by Alfred Noyes, copyright 1913.

THE YALE UNIVERSITY PRESS for "Prayer" by John Farrar.

THE WOMAN's PRESS for "The Kings of the East," "The Lame Shepherd" and "Christmas After War" from *The Pilgrim Ship* by Katherine Lee Bates.

Thanks are also due to the following magazines:

THE CENTURY MAGAZINE for "The Shepherd Who Stayed" by Theodosia Garrison.

GOOD HOUSEKEEPING for "Christmas Trees" by Violet Alleyn Storey.

HOLLAND'S MAGAZINE for "How Can They Honor Him" by Anderson M. Scruggs.

THE COMMONWEAL for "The Creche" by Carol Ryrie Brink.

THE GOLDEN BOOK for "Christmas" by Catherine Parmenter.

THE LADIES' HOME JOURNAL for "The Deathless Tale" by Charles Hanson Towne, copyright 1929, C. P. Co.; and "The Lord Christ Came to Notre Dame" by Richard Le Gallienne, copyright 1928, C. P. Co.

THE OUTLOOK for "The Haughty Aspen" by Nora Archibald Smith.

THE PARENTS' MAGAZINE for "Oh, Bring Not Gold" by Violet Alleyn Storey.

THE PICTORIAL REVIEW for "Bethlehem" (from an old French carol) by Bliss Carman.

THE SAINT NICHOLAS for "Song of the Christmas Trees" by Blanche Elizabeth Wade; "Christmas Eve" by Mary Mapes Dodge; and "The Little Gray Lamb" by Archibald Beresford Sullivan.

THE SURVEY for "The Other Shepherd" by Margaret Widdemer.

THE WOMAN'S HOME COMPANION for "The Lame Shepherd" by Katherine Lee Bates.

The editor furthermore wishes to thank personally the following authors for their co-operation:

Acknowledgments

Mary Austin, Carol Ryrie Brink, Gelett Burgess, Countee Cullen, Grace Noll Crowell, Walter de la Mare, John Farrar, Margaret Deland, Theodosia Garrison, Ruth Guthrie Harding, Laurence Housman, R. S. Hawker, Julie M. Lippmann, Edwin Markham, David Morton, Catherine Parmenter, Lizette Woodworth Reese, Clinton Scollard, Edmund Hamilton Sears, 2nd, Stephen Sennett, Edward Shillito, Nora Archibald Smith, Violet Alleyn Storey, Sara Teasdale, Charles Hanson Towne, Nancy Byrd Turner, Margaret Widdemer and Clement Wood.

The editor desires also to thank Mrs. George Burgess for the use of "The Kings of the East" and "The Lame Shepherd" by Katherine Lee Bates; Mr. Arthur Crandall for "Wayside Music" by Charles Henry Crandall; Miss Mildred Harrington for selections from "Our Holidays in Poetry" by Harrington and Thomas. (H. W. Wilson, pub. 1929); Miss Pamela Hinkson for "Bethlehem" and "A Song for the Season" by Katharine Tynan; Mr. Charles A. Kelly for "His Birthday" by May Riley Smith; Mrs. Vachel Lindsay for "Star of My Heart" by Vachel Lindsay; Dr. Francis A. Litz for "The Lamb Child" by Father Tabb; Mr. Lionel Marks for "Song of the Shepherd Boy at Bethlehem" by Josephine Preston Peabody; Mr. Wilfred Meynell for "Unto Us a Son Is Given" by Alice Meynell and Mr. Herbert D. Ward for "The Little Mud-Sparrows" by Elizabeth Stuart Phelps.

Contents

I

OLD ENGLISH CAROLS

II

THE NATIVITY

Contents

III

HYMNS AND SONGS OF ADORATION

IV

AND THERE WERE SHEPHERDS

V

BEHOLD THERE CAME WISE MEN FROM
THE EAST

Contents

VI

THE BIRDS PRAISE HIM

VII

THE TREES PRAISE HIM

Contents

VIII

THE CHRISTMAS FEAST

IX

THE CHRIST CHILD AND KRISS KRINGLE

Contents

X

THE MESSAGE OF CHRISTMAS TO OUR OWN TIME

Contents xxiii

I

OLD ENGLISH CAROLS

He neither shall be born
In housen, nor in hall,
Nor in the place of Paradise,
But in an ox's stall.

THE CHERRY-TREE CAROL

As Joseph was a-walking,
    He heard an angel sing,
"This night shall be the birth-time
    Of Christ, the heavenly king.

"He neither shall be born
    In housen nor in hall,
Nor in the place of Paradise,
    But in an ox's stall.

"He neither shall be clothèd
    In purple nor in pall,
But in the fair white linen
    That usen babies all.

"He neither shall be rockèd
    In silver nor in gold,
But in a wooden manger
    That resteth on the mould."

As Joseph was a-walking,
    There did an angel sing,
And Mary's child at midnight
    Was born to be our King.

Then be ye glad, good people,
   This night of all the year,
And light ye up your candles,
   For His star it shineth clear.

Old English

I SING OF A MAIDEN

I sing of a maiden
   That is makèless,[1]
King of all kings
   To her Son she ches.[2]

He came all so still
   Where His mother was,
As dew in April
   That falleth on the grass.

He came all so still
   Where His mother lay,
As dew in April
   That falleth on the spray.

He came all so still
   To His mother's bower,
As dew in April
   That falleth on the flower.

---

[1] makèless—matchless
[2] ches—chose

Mother and maiden
Was never none but she!
Well might such a lady
God's mother be.

Old Carol Attributed to Martin Shaw

GOD REST YE, MERRY GENTLEMEN

God rest ye, merry gentlemen; let nothing you dismay,
For Jesus Christ, our Saviour, was born on Christmas-
day.
The dawn rose red o'er Bethlehem, the stars shone
through the gray,
When Jesus Christ, our Saviour, was born on Christmas-
day.

God rest ye, little children; let nothing you affright,
For Jesus Christ, your Saviour, was born this happy
night;
Along the hills of Galilee the white flocks sleeping lay,
When Christ, the child of Nazareth, was born on
Christmas-day.

God rest ye, all good Christians; upon this blessèd
morn
The Lord of all good Christians was of a woman born;
Now all your sorrows He doth heal, your sins He takes
away;
For Jesus Christ, our Saviour, was born on Christmas-
day.

*Old English Carol adapted by Dinah Maria Mulock
Craik*

THE BURNING BABE

As I in hoary winter's night
   Stood shivering in the snow,
Surprised I was with sudden heat
   Which made my heart to glow;
And lifting up a fearful eye
   To view what fire was near,
A pretty babe all burning bright
   Did in the air appear:
Who, scorchèd with excessive heat,
   Such floods of tears did shed
As though His floods would quench His flames
   With which His tears were bred:
"Alas!" quoth He, "but newly born
   In fiery heats I fry,
Yet none approach to warm their hearts
   Or feel my fire but I.

"My faultless breast the furnace is;
   The fuel wounding thorns;
Love is the fire, and sighs the smoke;
   The ashes, shames and scorns;
The fuel Justice layeth on,
   And Mercy blows the coals,
The metal in this furnace wrought
   Are men's defilèd souls:
For which, as now on fire I am
   To work them for their good,
So will I melt into a bath,
   To wash them in my blood."

With this He vanish'd out of sight
And swiftly shrunk away,
And straight I callèd unto mind
That it was Christmas Day.

Robert Southwell

I SAW THREE SHIPS

I saw three ships come sailing in
On Christmas day, on Christmas day;
I saw three ships come sailing in
On Christmas day in the morning.

And what was in those ships all three
On Christmas day, on Christmas day?
And what was in those ships all three
On Christmas day in the morning?

The Virgin Mary and Christ were there
On Christmas day, on Christmas day;
The Virgin Mary and Christ were there
On Christmas day in the morning.

Pray whither sailed those ships all three
On Christmas day, on Christmas day?
Pray whither sailed those ships all three
On Christmas day in the morning?

O, they sailed into Bethlehem
On Christmas day, on Christmas day;
O, they sailed into Bethlehem
On Christmas day in the morning.

And all the bells on earth shall ring
   On Christmas day, on Christmas day;
And all the bells on earth shall ring
   On Christmas day in the morning.

And all the angels in Heaven shall sing
   On Christmas day, on Christmas day;
And all the angels in Heaven shall sing
   On Christmas day in the morning.

And all the souls on earth shall sing
   On Christmas day, on Christmas day;
And all the souls on earth shall sing
   On Christmas day in the morning.

Then let us all rejoice amain
   On Christmas day, on Christmas day;
Then let us all rejoice amain
   On Christmas day in the morning.
               Old English Carol

THE GOLDEN CAROL OF MELCHIOR, BAL-THAZAR AND GASPAR, THE THREE KINGS

We saw the light shine out a-far,
   On Christmas in the morning.
And straight we knew Christ's Star it was,
   Bright beaming in the morning.

Then did we fall on bended knee,
  On Christmas in the morning,
And prais'd the Lord, who'd let us see
  His glory at its dawning.

Oh! every thought be of His Name,
  On Christmas in the morning,
Who bore for us both grief and shame,
  Afflictions sharpest scorning.
And may we die (when death shall come),
  On Christmas in the morning,
And see in Heav'n, our glorious home,
  The Star of Christmas morning.

                    Old English

POVERTY

All poor men and humble,
All lame men who stumble,
  Come haste ye, nor feel ye afraid;
For Jesus, our treasure,
With love past all measure,
  In lowly poor manger was laid.

Though wise men who found Him
Laid rich gifts around Him,
  Yet oxen they gave Him their hay:
And Jesus in beauty
Accepted their duty;
  Contented in manger He lay.

Then haste we to show Him
The praises we owe Him;
    Our service He ne'er can despise:
Whose love still is able
To show us that stable
    Where softly in manger He lies.
Old Welsh Carol Translated by K. E. Roberts

SAINT STEPHEN WAS A CLERK

Saint Stephen was a clerk in King Herod's hall,
And servèd him of bread and cloth, as ever king befall.

Stephen out of kitchen came with boar's head in (his)
    hand,
He saw a star (that) was fair and bright over Bethlehem
    stand.

He cast adown the boar's head and went into the hall:
"I forsake thee, King Herod, and thy workës all.

"I forsake thee, King Herod, and thy workës all;
There is a child in Bethlehem born is better than we
    all."

"What aileth thee, Stephen, what is thee befall?
Lacketh thee either meat or drink in King Herod's
    hall?"

"Lacketh me neither meat nor drink in King Herod's
    hall,

There is a child in Bethlehem born is better than we
    all."

"What aileth thee, Stephen, art thou mad, or thou
    ginnest to brede? [1]
Lacketh thee either gold or fee or any richë weed?"

"Lacketh me neither gold nor fee, nor no richë weed,
There is a child in Bethlehem born shall help us at our
    need."

"That is all so sooth, Stephen, all so sooth ywis,
As this capon crow (it) shall, that lieth here in my
    dish."

That word was not so soonë said, that word in that hall,
The capon crew, *Christus natus est*, among the lordës
    all.
"Riseth up my tormentors, by twos and all by one,
And leadeth Stephen out of this town, and stoneth him
    with stone."

Took (they then) Stephen and stoned him in the way,
Therefore is his even on Christës own day.

Anonymous
Fifteenth Century

---

[1] rave

II

THE NATIVITY

The time draws near the birth of Christ.

THE TIME DRAWS NEAR THE BIRTH OF CHRIST

The time draws near the birth of Christ:
    The moon is hid; the night is still;
    The Christmas bells from hill to hill
Answer each other in the mist.

Four voices of four hamlets round,
    From far and near, on mead and moor,
    Swell out and fail, as if a door
Were shut between me and the sound.

Each voice four changes on the wind.
    That now dilate, and now decrease,
    Peace and goodwill, goodwill and peace,
Peace and goodwill, to all mankind.

                                    Alfred Tennyson

MARY'S GIRLHOOD

This is the blessèd Mary, pre-elect
    God's virgin. Gone is a great while, and she
    Dwelt young in Nazareth of Galilee.
Unto God's will she brought devout respect,
Profound simplicity of intellect.
    And supreme patience. From her mother's knee
    Faithful and hopeful; wise in charity;
Strong in grave peace; in pity circumspect.

So held she through her girlhood; as it were
An angel-watered lily, that near God
Grows and is quiet. Till, one day at home,
She woke in her white bed, and had no fear
At all, yet wept till sunshine, and felt awed:
Because the fullness of the time was near.

Dante Gabriel Rossetti

BETHLEHEM

Long was the road to Bethlehem,
Where Joseph and his Mary came.
They are travel-worn, the day grows late,
As they reach the town with its towered gate—
The city of David's royal line—
And the stars of eve are beginning to shine.
They must seek a place where the poor may rest,
For Mary is weary and overpressed.

AND IT IS THE SIXTH HOUR.

They come to an inn and knock on the door,
Asking a little space,—no more
Than a humble shelter in their need.
The innkeeper gives them scanty heed.
Little for strangers does he care—
His house is full. They must seek elsewhere.
Fearing to find no place that day,
Heavy at heart they turn away.

AND IT IS THE SEVENTH HOUR.

In weariness and sore perplexed,
To a larger house they venture next.

Joseph for pity's sake begs again
A lodging for Mary in her pain.
They are poor Galileans, plain to be told—
Their garments are worn, their sandals are old.
The fat innkeeper jingles his keys,
And refuses shelter to such as these.

AND IT IS THE NINTH HOUR.

Where now they turn the woman is kind,
The place is crowded, still she would find
Room for them somehow—moved at the sight
Of this gentle girl in her urgent plight,
Who tells of her hope and her strength far spent,
And seems to her woman's heart God-sent,
But the surly landlord roars in wrath
And sends them forth on their lonely path.

AND IT IS THE ELEVENTH HOUR.

Still seeking a place to lay them down,
They come at length, on the edge of the town,
To a cattle-shed with sagging door,
Thankful for only the stable floor,
When an old gray donkey crowds to the wall
To make them room in his straw-laid stall.
And the cattle low at the stifled wail
Of a woman's voice in sore travail.

IT IS MIDNIGHT AND MARY'S HOUR.

Over the place a great new star
Sheds wonder and glory beheld afar,
While all through the height of heaven there flies

The word of a seraph voice that cries,
"Glory to God, this wondrous morn
On earth the Saviour Christ is born."

Bliss Carman
(*From old French Carol adapted by Yvette Guilbert.*)

A CHRISTMAS SONG

When from His throne the Godhead bowed
    To human form below,
The Heavens dropt down, and every cloud
    Hung loath to let Him go.
Oh, bright the light, and white the night,
    When, full of favour stored,
God's Maid lay down in Bethlehem town,
    To wait the coming Lord!

Before His Feet went down the snow
    Amid the tranquil night,
Till all the world lay white below
    To greet the Lord of Light.
Oh, bright the light, and white the night,
    When, full of favour stored,
God's Maid lay down in Bethlehem town,
    To wait the coming Lord!

The rugged hills and all the rocks
    Where covered as with fleece;
The towns were seen like folded flocks
    To wait the Prince of Peace.

Oh, bright the light, and white the night,
  When, full of favour stored,
God's Maid lay down in Bethlehem town,
  To wait the coming Lord!

Oh, like a flock in field and fold,
  The wintry world lay then,
On that fair night in days of old
  When Christ came down to men.
Oh, bright the light, and white the night,
  When, full of favour stored,
God's Maid lay down in Bethlehem town,
  To wait the coming Lord!

Laurence Housman

TRYSTE NOËL

The Ox he openeth wide the Doore,
And from the Snowe he calls her inne,
And he hath seen her Smile therefor,
Our Ladye without Sinne.
Now soone from Sleep
A Starre shall leap,
And soone arrive both King and Hinde:
  Amen, Amen:
But O, the Place co'd I but finde!

The Ox hath hush'd his voyce and bent
Trewe eyes of Pitty ore the Mow,
And on his lovelie Neck, forspent,
The Blessed layes her Browe.

Around her feet
Full Warme and Sweete
His bowerie Breath doth meeklie dwell:
  Amen, Amen:
But sore am I with Vaine Travel!

The Ox is host in Judah stall
The Host of more than onelie one,
For close she gathereth withal
Our Lord her littel Sonne.
Glad Hinde and King
Their Gyfte may bring,
And wo'd to-night my Teares were there,
  Amen, Amen:
Between her Bosom and His Hayre!

                    Louise Imogen Guiney

WE SAW HIM SLEEPING

We saw Him sleeping in His manger bed
And faltered feet and heart in holy dread.
Until we heard the maiden-mother call:
"Come hither, sirs, He is so sweet and small."

She was more fair than ye have looked upon,
She was the moon and He her little sun;
"O Lord," we cried, "have mercy on us all!"
"But ah," quod she, "He is so sweet and small."

Whereat the blessèd beasts with one accord,
Gave tongue to praise their little blessèd Lord,
Oxen and asses singing in their stall:
"The King of Kings He is so sweet and small."
                    From the Old English

NEW PRINCE, NEW POMP

Behold a little, tender Babe,
In freezing winter night,
In homely manger trembling lies;
Alas! a piteous sight.
The inns are full; no man will yield
This little Pilgrim bed;
But forced He is with silly beasts
In crib to shroud His head.

Weigh not His crib, His wooden dish,
Nor beasts that by Him feed;
Weigh not His mother's poor attire,
Nor Joseph's simple weed.
This stable is a Prince's court,
This crib His chair of state;
The beasts are parcel of His pomp,
The wooden dish His plate.

The persons in that poor attire
His royal liv'ries wear;
The Prince Himself is come from Heav'n;
This pomp is praised there.

With joy approach, O Christian wight!
Do homage to thy King;
And highly praise this humble pomp,
Which He from Heav'n doth bring.

Robert Southwell

BETHLEHEM

Where man was all too marred with sin,
The ass, the ox were bidden in.

Where angels were unmeet to come,
The humble entered Holydom.

Their innocent eyes, and full of awe,
Saw the fulfillment of the Law.

There, in the stable with the beast,
The Christmas Child hath spread His feast.

These gave their bread and eke their board
To be a cradle for their Lord.

Their honey-breath, their tears all mild,
Warmed in the cold the new-born Child.

These His adorers were before
The Kings and Shepherds thronged the door.

And where no angels knelt there kneeled
The innocent creatures of the field.

O simple ones, much honorèd;
He who oppresses you indeed,

Oppresses His kind hosts that lay
Once in the stable on the hay.
Katharine Tynan

CHRISTMAS FOLKSONG

The little Jesus came to town;
The wind blew up, the wind blew down;
Out in the street the wind was bold;
Now who would house Him from the cold?

Then opened wide a stable door
Fain were the rushes on the floor;
The Ox put forth a hornèd head:
"Come, little Lord, here make Thy bed."

Uprose the Sheep were folded near:
"Thou Lamb of God, come, enter here."
He entered there to rush and reed,
Who was the Lamb of God indeed.

The little Jesus came to town;
With ox and sheep He laid Him down.
Peace to the byre, peace to the fold,
For that they housed Him from the cold.
Lizette Woodworth Reese

THE OXEN

Christmas Eve, and twelve of the clock.
"Now they are all on their knees,"
An elder said as we sat in a flock
By the embers in hearthside ease.

We pictured the meek, mild creatures where
They dwelt in their strawy pen,
Nor did it occur to one of us there
To doubt they were kneeling then.

So fair a fancy few would weave
In these years! Yet, I feel,
If someone said on Christmas Eve,
"Come, see the oxen kneel

"In the lonely barton by yonder coomb
Our childhood used to know,"
I should go with him in the gloom
Hoping it might be so.

Thomas Hardy

ATTENDANTS

The mild-eyed Oxen and the gentle Ass,
  By manger or in pastures that they graze,
Lift their slow heads to watch us where we pass,
  A reminiscent wonder in their gaze.

Their low humility is like a crown,
   A grave distinction they have come to wear,—
Their look gone past us—to a little Town,
And a white miracle that happened there.

An old, old vision haunts those quiet eyes,
   Where proud remembrance drifts to them again,
Of Something that has made them humbly wise,
   These burden-bearers for the race of men—
And lightens every load they lift or pull,
Something that chanced because the Inn was full.

                      David Morton

GATES AND DOORS—A BALLAD OF CHRISTMAS EVE

There was a gentle hostler
   (And blessèd be his name!)
He opened up the stable
   The night Our Lady came.
Our Lady and Saint Joseph,
   He gave them food and bed,
And Jesus Christ has given him
   A glory round his head.

    So let the gate swing open
      However poor the yard,
    Lest weary people visit you
      And find their passage barred.

Unlatch the door at midnight
And let your lantern's glow
Shine out to guide the traveller's feet
To you across the snow.

There was a courteous hostler
  (He is in Heaven tonight!)
He held Our Lady's bridle
  And helped her to alight.
He spread clean straw before her
  Whereon she might lie down,
And Jesus Christ has given him
  An everlasting crown.

Unlock the door this evening
  And let the gate swing wide,
Let all who ask for shelter
  Come speedily inside.
What if your yard be narrow?
  What if your house be small?
There is a Guest is coming
  Will glorify it all.

There was a joyous hostler
  Who knelt on Christmas morn
Beside the radiant manger
  Wherein his Lord was born.
His heart was full of laughter,
  His soul was full of bliss
When Jesus, on His mother's lap,
  Gave him His hand to kiss.

Unbar your heart this evening
And keep no stranger out,
Take from your soul's great portal
The barrier of doubt.
To humble folk and weary
Give hearty welcoming,
Your breast shall be tomorrow
The cradle of a King.

                    Joyce Kilmer

THE LITTLE TOWN

O little town, O little town,
Upon the hills so far,
We see you, like a thing sublime,
Across the great gray wastes of time,
And men go up and men go down,
But follow still the star!

And this is humble Bethlehem
In the Judean wild;
And this is lowly Bethlehem
Wherein a mother smiled;
Yea, this is happy Bethlehem
That knew the little Child!

Aye, this is glorious Bethlehem
Where He drew living breath
(Ah, precious, precious Bethlehem!—
So every mortal saith.)
Who brought to all that tread the earth
Life's triumph over death!

O little town, O little town,
  Upon the hills afar,
You call to us, a thing sublime,
  Across the great gray wastes of time,
For men go up and men go down,
  But follow still the star!

Clinton Scollard

HOW FAR IS IT TO BETHLEHEM

How far is it to Bethlehem?
  Not very far.
Shall we find the stable-room
  Lit by a star?

Can we see the little Child?
  Is He within?
If we lift the wooden latch
  May we go in?

May we stroke the creatures there,
  Ox, ass, or sheep?
May we peep like them and see
  Jesus asleep?

If we touch His tiny hand
  Will He awake?
Will He know we've come so far
  Just for His sake?

Great Kings have precious gifts,
    And we have naught;
Little smiles and little tears
    Are all we brought.

For all weary children
    Mary must weep.
Here, on His bed of straw,
    Sleep, children, sleep.

God in His Mother's arms
    Babes in the byre,
Sleep, as they sleep who find
    Their heart's desire.

Frances Chesterton

O LITTLE TOWN OF BETHLEHEM

O little town of Bethlehem!
How still we see thee lie;
Above thy deep and dreamless sleep
The silent stars go by;
Yet in thy dark streets shineth
The everlasting Light;
The hopes and fears of all the years
Are met in thee tonight.

For Christ is born of Mary,
And gathered all above,
While mortals sleep, the angels keep
Their watch ·of wond'ring love.

O morning stars, together
Proclaim the holy birth!
And praises sing to God the King,
And peace to men on earth!

How silently, how silently
The wondrous gift is given!
So God imparts to human hearts
The blessings of His heaven.
No ear may hear His coming,
But in this world of sin,
Where meek souls will receive Him still,
The dear Christ enters in.

O holy Child of Bethlehem!
Descend to us, we pray;
Cast out our sin, and enter in,
Be born in us today.
We hear the Christmas angels,
The great glad tidings tell;
O come to us, abide with us,
Our Lord Emmanuel!

Phillips Brooks

CHRISTMAS SONG

Calm on the listening ear of night
    Come heaven's melodious strains,
Where wild Judea stretches far
    Her silver-mantled plains;

Celestial choirs from courts above
    Shed sacred glories there;
And angels with their sparkling lyres
    Make music on the air.

The answering hills of Palestine
    Send back the glad reply,
And greet from all their holy heights
    The day-spring from on high:
O'er the blue depths of Galilee
    There comes a holier calm,
And Sharon waves, in solemn praise,
    Her silent groves of palm.

"Glory to God!" The lofty strain
    The realm of ether fills:
How sweeps the song of solemn joy
    O'er Judah's sacred hills!
"Glory to God!" The sounding skies
    Loud with their anthems ring;
"Peace on the earth; good-will to men,
    From heaven's eternal King!"

Light on thy hills, Jerusalem!
    The Saviour now is born:
More bright on Bethlehem's joyous plains
    Breaks the first Christmas morn:
And brighter on Moriah's brow,
    Crowned with her temple-spires,
Which first proclaim the new-born light,
    Clothed with its Orient fires.

This day shall Christian lips be mute,
And Christian hearts be cold?
Oh, catch the anthem that from heaven
O'er Judah's mountains rolled!
When nightly burst from seraph-harps
The high and solemn lay,—
"Glory to God! on earth be peace;
Salvation comes to-day!"

Edmund Hamilton Sears

III

HYMNS AND SONGS OF ADORATION

O come let us adore Him.

ADESTE FIDELES

Adeste fideles. Laeti triumphantes:
Venite, venite in Bethlehem.
Natum videte, Regem angelorum,
Venite, adoremus, venite, adoremus:
Venite, adoremus Dominum.

Deum de Deo, Lumen de lumine
Gestant puellae viscera
Deum verum, genitum, non factum,
Venite, adoremus, venite, adoremus:
Venite, adoremus Dominum.

Cantet nunc Io chorus angelorum.
Cantet aula celestium
Gloria, gloria, in excelsis Deo
Venite, adoremus, venite, adoremus:
Venite, adoremus Dominum.

Ergo, qui natus die hodierna
Jesu tibi sit gloria:
Patris aeterim Verbum caro factum,
Venite, adoremus, venite, adoremus:
Venite, adoremus Dominum.

M. Portugal

O COME, ALL YE FAITHFUL

O come, all ye faithful, joyful and triumphant;
O come ye, O come ye to Bethlehem;
Come and behold Him, born the King of angels:
O come let us adore Him, O come let us adore Him,
O come let us adore Him, Christ the Lord.

God of God, Light of Light,
Lo! He abhors not the Virgin's womb;
Very God, begotten not created:
O come let us adore Him, O come let us adore Him,
O come let us adore Him, Christ the Lord.

Sing, choirs of angels, sing in exultation,—
Sing, all ye citizens of heaven above:
Glory to God, in the highest glory:
O come let us adore Him, O come let us adore Him,
O come let us adore Him, Christ the Lord.

Yea, Lord, we greet Thee,
Born this happy morning;—
Jesus, to Thee be glory given;
Word of the Father, now in flesh appearing:
O come let us adore Him, O come let us adore Him,
O come let us adore Him, Christ the Lord.

Translated by Rev. F. Oakeley

STILLE NACHT, HEILIGE NACHT
Altes Weihnachtslied

Stille Nacht, heilige Nacht,
Alles schläft, einsam wacht
Nur das traute hochheilige Paar.
Holder Knabe in lockigen Haar,
Schlaf' in himmlischer Ruh',
Schlaf' in himmlischer Ruh'.

Stille Nacht, heilige Nacht,
Hirten erst kund gemacht
Durch der Engel Halleluja,
Tönt es laut von fern und nah:
Christ der Retter is da!
Christ der Retter is da!

Stille Nacht, heilige Nacht,
Gottessohn, o wie lacht
Lieb' aus deinem göttlichen Mund,
Da uns schlägt die rettende Stund',
Christ, in deiner Geburt!
Christ, in deiner Geburt!

SILENT NIGHT

Silent night, holy night,
All is calm, all is bright
Round yon Virgin Mother and Child,
Holy Infant so tender and mild,
Sleep in heavenly peace,
Sleep in heavenly peace!

Silent night, holy night,
Shepherds quake at the sight,
Glories stream from heaven afar,
Heav'nly hosts sing Alleluia;
Christ, the Saviour is born,
Christ, the Saviour is born!

Silent night, holy night,
Son of God, love's pure light
Radiant beams from Thy holy face,
With the dawn of redeeming grace,
Jesus, Lord, at Thy birth,
Jesus, Lord at Thy birth.

Franz Gruber

A HYMN OF THE NATIVITY

I sing the birth was born to-night,
The author both of life and light;
   The angels so did sound it.
And like the ravished shepherds said,
Who saw the light and were afraid,
   Yet searched, and true they found it.

The Son of God, th' Eternal King,
That did us all salvation bring,
   And freed the soul from danger;
He whom the whole world could not take,
The Word, which heaven and earth did make,
   Was now laid in a manger.

The Father's wisdom willed it so,
The Son's obedience knew no No,
    Both wills were in one stature;
And as that wisdom had decreed,
The Word was now made Flesh indeed,
    And took on Him our Nature.

What comfort by Him do we win,
Who made Himself the price of sin,
    To make us heirs of Glory?
To see this babe, all innocence,
A martyr born in our defence,
    Can man forget this story?

Ben Jonson

ON THE MORNING OF CHRIST'S NATIVITY

This is the month, and this the happy morn,
Wherein the Son of Heaven's eternal King,
Of wedded maid and virgin-mother born,
Our great redemption from above did bring;
For so the holy sages once did sing,
    That He our deadly forfeit should release,
And with His Father work us a perpetual peace.

That glorious Form, that Light unsufferable,
And that far-beaming Blaze of Majesty,
Wherewith He wont at Heaven's high council-table
To sit the midst of Trinal Unity.
He laid aside; and, here with us to be,
    Forsook the courts of everlasting day,
And chose with us a darksome house of mortal clay.

Say, heavenly Muse, shall not thy sacred vein
Afford a present to the Infant God?
Hast thou no verse, no hymn, or solemn strain,
To welcome Him to this His new abode,
Now while the heaven, by the sun's team untrod,
   Hath took no print of the approaching light,
And all the spangled host kept watch in squadrons
     bright?

See, how from far, upon the eastern road,
The star-led wizards haste with odours sweet;
O run, prevent them with thy humble ode,
And lay it lowly at His blessèd feet;
Have thou the honour first thy Lord to greet,
   And join thy voice unto the Angel quire,
From out His secret altar touch'd with hallow'd fire.

John Milton

HARK! THE HERALD ANGELS SING

Hark! the herald angels sing,
Glory to the new-born King;
Peace on earth and mercy mild,
God and sinners reconciled!
Joyful, all ye nations, rise,
Join the triumph of the skies;
With the angelic host proclaim,
Christ is born in Bethlehem.
Hark! the herald angels sing,
Glory to the new-born King.

Christ, by highest heav'n adored;
Christ, the everlasting Lord;
Late in time behold Him come,
Off-spring of the Virgin's womb.
Veiled in flesh the God-head see;
Hail the incarnate Deity,—
Pleased as Man with man to dwell,
Jesus, our Emmanuel!
Hark! the herald angels sing,
Glory to the new-born King.

Mild He lays His glory by,—
Born that man no more may die,
Born to raise the sons of earth,
Born to give them second birth,
Risen with healing in His wings,
Light and life to all He brings,
Hail, the Sun of Righteousness!
Hail, the heaven-born Prince of Peace!
Hark! the herald angels sing,
Glory to the new-born King.

Charles Wesley

BRIGHTEST AND BEST OF THE SONS OF THE MORNING

Brightest and best of the sons of the morning,
  Dawn on our darkness, and lend us thine aid!
Star of the East, the horizon adorning,
  Guide where our infant Redeemer is laid!

Cold on His cradle the dew-drops are shining;
　Low lies His head with the beasts of the stall:
Angels adore Him, in slumber reclining,
　Maker and Monarch and Saviour of all.

Say, shall we yield Him, in costly devotion,
　Odours of Edom and offerings divine?
Gems of the mountains and pearls of the ocean,
　Myrrh from the forest, or gold from the mine?

Vainly we offer each ample oblation:
　Vainly with gifts would His favour secure;
Richer by far is the heart's adoration;
　Dearer to God are the prayers of the poor.

Brightest and best of the sons of the morning,
　Dawn on our darkness, and lend us thine aid!
Star of the east, the horizon adorning,
　Guide where our infant Redeemer is laid!

Reginald Heber

IT CAME UPON THE MIDNIGHT CLEAR

It came upon the midnight clear,
That glorious song of old,
From angels bending near the earth,
To touch their harps of gold:
"Peace on the earth, goodwill to men
From heaven's all gracious King."
The world in solemn stillness lay
To hear the angels sing.

Still through the cloven skies they come,
With peaceful wings unfurled;
And still their heavenly music floats
O'er all the weary world:
Above its sad and lonely plains
They bend on hovering wing.
And ever o'er its Babel sounds
The blessèd angels sing.

O ye, beneath life's crushing load,
Whose forms are bending low,
Who toil along the climbing way
With painful steps and slow!
Look now, for glad and golden hours
Come swiftly on the wing:
O rest beside the weary road,
And hear the angels sing.

For lo, the days are hastening on
By prophet bards foretold,
When with the ever circling years
Comes round the Age of Gold;
When Peace shall over all the earth
Its ancient splendors fling,
And the whole world give back the song
Which now the angels sing.

                    Edmund Hamilton Sears

THE FIRST NOWELL

The first Nowell the angel did say
Was to certain poor shepherds in fields as they lay;
In fields where they lay keeping their sheep
On a cold winter's night that was so deep.
Nowell, Nowell, Nowell, Nowell,—Born is the King
        of Israel.

They looked up and saw a Star,
Shining in the East, beyond them far,
And to the earth it gave great light,
And so it continued both day and night.
Nowell, Nowell, Nowell, Nowell,—Born is the King
        of Israel.

This Star drew nigh to the north-west,
O'er Bethlehem it took its rest,
And there it did both stop and stay
Right over the place where Jesus lay.
Nowell, Nowell, Nowell, Nowell,—Born is the King
        of Israel.

Then entered in there Wise Men three,
Full rev'rently upon their knee,
And offer'd there in His presence
Their gold and myrrh and frankincense.
Nowell, Nowell, Nowell, Nowell,—Born is the King
        of Israel.

Old Song

WHILE SHEPHERDS WATCHED

While shepherds watched their flocks by night,
   All seated on the ground,
The angel of the Lord came down,
   And glory shone around.

"Fear not," said he,—for mighty dread
   Had seized their troubled mind,
"Glad tidings of great joy I bring
   To you and all mankind.

"To you in David's town this day
   Is born of David's line,
A Saviour, who is Christ the Lord;
   And this shall be the sign:

"The heavenly Babe you there shall find
   To human view displayed,
All meanly wrapt in swathing bands,
   And in a manger laid."

Thus spake the seraph, and forthwith
   Appeared a shining throng
Of angels praising God, and thus
   Addressed their joyful song:

"All glory be to God on high,
   And to the earth be peace;
Good-will henceforth from heaven to men
   Begin and never cease!"

Nahum Tate

IV

AND THERE WERE SHEPHERDS

The first Nowell the angels did say
Was to certain poor shepherds in fields as they lay.

THE JOLLY SHEPHERD WAT

The shepherd upon a hill he sat,
He had on him his tabard [1] and his hat,
His tar-box, his pipe and his flagat,[2]
His name was called jolly, jolly Wat;
For he was a good herd's boy,
    Ut Hoy!
For in his pipe he made so much joy.
  Can I not sing but hoy,
   When the jolly shepherd made so much joy.

The shepherd upon a hill was laid,
His dog to his girdle was tied;
He had not slept but a little braid,[3]
But *"Gloria in excelsis"* was to him said.
    Ut Hoy!
For in his pipe he made so much joy.
  Can I not sing but hoy,
   When the jolly shepherd made so much joy.

The shepherd on a hill he stood,
Round about him his sheep they yode;[4]
He put his hand under his hood,
He saw a star as red as blood.

---

[1] short coat.
[2] bottle.
[3] time.
[4] went.

Ut Hoy!
For in his pipe he made so much joy.
Can I not sing but hoy,
When the jolly shepherd made so much joy.

"Now farewell Mall and also Will,
For my love, go ye all still
Unto[5] I come again you till,[6]
And evermore, Will, ring well thy bell."
        Ut Hoy!
For in his pipe he made so much joy.
Can I not sing but hoy,
When the jolly shepherd made so much joy.

"Now must I go where Christ was born;
Farewell! I come again to-morn.
Dog, keep well my sheep from the corn,
And warn well Warrock when I blow my horn."
        Ut Hoy!
For in his pipe he made so much joy.
Can I not sing but hoy,
When the jolly shepherd made so much joy.

When Wat to Bethlehem comë was,
He sweat; he had gone faster than a pace;
He found Jesus in a simple place,
Between an ox and an .ass.

---

[5] until.
[6] to.

Ut Hoy!
For in his pipe he made so much joy.
  Can I not sing but hoy,
  When the jolly shepherd made so much joy.

The shepherd said anon right:
"I will go see yon ferly [7] sight,
Whereas the angel singeth on height,
And the star that shineth so bright."
        Ut Hoy!
For in his pipe he made so much joy.
  Can I not sing but hoy,
  When the jolly shepherd made so much joy.

"Jesu! I offer to Thee here my pipe,
My scrip, my tar-box, and my skirt;
Home to my fellows now will I skip,
And also look unto my sheep."
        Ut Hoy!
For in his pipe he made so much joy.
  Can I not sing but hoy,
  When the jolly shepherd made so much joy.

"Now farewell, my own herdsman Wat!"
"Yea, for God, Lady, even so I hight,[8]
Lull well Jesu in thy lap,
And farewell, Joseph, with thy round cape!"

---

[7] strange.
[8] am called.

Ut Hoy!
For in his pipe he made so much joy.
Can I not sing but hoy,
When the jolly shepherd made so much joy.

"Now may I well both hope and sing,
For I have been at Christ's bearing;
Home to my fellows now will I fling;
Christ of heaven to His bliss us bring!"
Ut Hoy!
For in his pipe he made so much joy.
Can I not sing but hoy,
When the jolly shepherd made so much joy.
Ancient Carol

BOOTS AND SADDLES

Our shepherds all
    As pilgrims have departed,
Our shepherds all
    Have gone to Bethlehem.
They gladly go,
    For they are all stout-hearted,
They gladly go—
    Ah, could I go with them!

I am too lame to walk,
    Boots and saddles, boots and saddles,
I am too lame to walk,
    Boots and saddles, mount and ride.

A shepherd stout
 Who sang a catamiaulo,
A shepherd stout
 Was walking lazily.
He heard me speak and saw me hobbling
  after,
He turned and said
 He would give help to me.

"Here is my horse
 That flies along the high-road.
Here is my horse,
 The best in all the towns.
I bought him from
 A soldier in the army,
I got my horse
 By payment of five crowns."

When I have seen
 The Child, the King of Heaven,
When I have seen
 The Child who is God's Son.
When to the mother,
 I my praise have given,
When I have finished,
 All I should have done:

No more shall I be lame,
 Boots and saddles, boots and saddles,
No more shall I be lame,
 Boots and saddles, mount and ride.
          Provençal Noël of Nicholas Saboly

THE STORY OF THE SHEPHERD

It was the very noon of night; the stars above the fold,
More sure than clock or chiming bell, the hour of
    midnight told:
When from the heav'ns there came a voice, and forms
    were seen to shine
Still bright'ning as the music rose with light and love
    divine.
With love divine, the song began: there shone a light
    serene:
O, who hath heard what I have heard, or seen what I
    have seen?

O ne'er could nightingale at dawn salute the rising day
With sweetness like that bird of song in his immortal
    lay:
O ne'er were woodnotes heard at eve by banks with
    poplar shade
So thrilling as the concert sweet by heav'nly harpings
    made;
For love divine was in each chord, and filled each
    pause between:
O, who hath heard what I have heard, or seen what I
    have seen?

I roused me at the piercing strain, but shrunk as from
    the ray
Of summer lightning: all around so bright the splendor
    lay.
For oh, it mastered sight and sense, to see that glory
    shine,

To hear that minstrel in the clouds, who sang of
    Love Divine.
To see that form with bird-like wings, of more than
    mortal mien:
O, who hath heard what I have heard, or seen what I
    have seen?

When once the rapturous trance was past, that so my
    sense could blind,
I left my sheep to Him whose care breathed in the
    western wind:
I left them, for instead of snow, I trod on blade and
    flower,
And ice dissolved in starry rays at morning's gracious
    hour,
Revealing where on earth the steps of Love Divine
    had been:
O, who hath heard what I have heard, or seen what I
    have seen?

I hasted to a low-roofed shed, for so the Angel bade;
And bowed before the lowly rack where Love Divine
    was laid:
A new-born Babe, like tender Lamb, with Lion's
    strength there smiled;
For Lion's strength immortal might, was in that new-
    born Child:
That Love Divine in child-like form had God forever
    been:
O, who hath heard what I have heard, or seen what I
    have seen?

Translated from the Spanish

SHEPHERDS REJOICE

"Shepherds, rejoice, lift up your eyes.
    And send your fears away;
News from the region of the skies!
    Salvation's born today.

"Jesus, the God whom Angels fear,
    Comes down to dwell with you;
Today He makes His entrance here,
    But not as monarchs do.

"No gold, nor purple swaddling-bands,
    Nor royal shining things;
A manger for His cradle stands,
    And holds the King of kings.

"Go, shepherds, where the Infant lies,
    And see His humble throne:
With tears of joy in all your eyes
    Go, shepherds, kiss the Son."

Thus Gabriel sang; and straight around
    The heavenly armies throng;
They tune their harps to lofty sound,
    And thus conclude the song:

"Glory to God that reigns above,
    Let peace surround the earth;
Mortals shall know their Maker's love
    At their Redeemer's birth."

Lord! and shall angels have their songs,
 And men no tunes to raise?
O may we lose these useless tongues
 When they forget to praise!

Glory to God that reigns above,
 That pitied us, forlorn!
We join to sing our Maker's love—
 For there's a Saviour born!

                                        Isaac Watts

A CHRISTMAS CAROL

"What means this glory round our feet,"
 The Magi mused, "more bright than morn?"
And voices chanted clear and sweet,
 "Today the Prince of Peace is born!"

"What means that star," the Shepherds said,
 "That brightens through the rocky glen?"
And angels, answering overhead,
 Sang, "Peace on earth, good-will to men!"

'Tis eighteen hundred years and more
 Since those sweet oracles were dumb;
We wait for Him, like them of yore;
 Alas, He seems so slow to come!

But it is said, in words of gold,
 No time or sorrow e'er shall dim,
That little children might be bold
 In perfect trust to come to Him.

All round about our feet shall shine
   A light like that the wise men saw,
If we our loving wills incline
   To that sweet Life which is the Law.

So shall we learn to understand
   The simple faith of shepherds then,
And, clasping kindly hand in hand,
   Sing, "Peace on earth, good-will to men!"

But they who do their souls no wrong,
   And keep at eve the faith of morn,
Shall daily hear the angel-song,
   "Today the Prince of Peace is born!"
                              James Russell Lowell

THE SHEPHERDS IN JUDEA

   Oh, the Shepherds in Judea
      They are pacing to and fro,
      For the air grows chill at twilight
      And the weanling lambs are slow!
Leave, O lambs, the dripping sedges, quit the bramble
      and the brier,
Leave the fields of barley stubble, for we light the
      watching-fire;
Twinkling fires across the twilight, and a bitter watch
      to keep,
Lest the prowlers come a-thieving where the flocks
      unguarded sleep.

Oh, the Shepherds in Judea
    They are singing soft and low—
  Song the blessèd angels taught them
    All the centuries ago!
There was never roof to hide them, there were never
    walls to bind;
Stark they lie beneath the star-beams, whom the blessed
    angels find,
With the huddled flocks upstarting, wondering if they
    hear aright,
While the Kings come riding, riding, solemn shadows
    in the night.

Oh, the Shepherds in Judea
    They are thinking, as they go,
  Of the light that broke their watching
    On the hillside in the snow!
Scattered snow along the hillside, white as springtime
    fleeces are,
With the whiter wings above them and the glory-
    streaming star—
Guiding-star across the housetops: never fear the Shep-
    herds felt
Till they found the Babe in manger where the kindly
    cattle knelt.

Oh, the Shepherds in Judea!—
    Do you think the Shepherds know
  How the whole round earth is brightened
    In the ruddy Christmas glow?

How the sighs are lost in laughter, and the laughter
    brings the tears,
As the thoughts of men go seeking back across the
    darkling years,
Till they find the wayside stable that the star-led
    Wise Men found,
With the Shepherds, mute, adoring, and the glory
    shining round!

Mary Austin

FROM FAR AWAY

"From far away we come to you.
    The snow in the street, and the wind on the door,
To tell of great tidings, strange and true.
    Minstrels and maids, stand forth on the floor.
      From far away we come to you,
        To tell of great tidings, strange and true.

"For as we wandered far and wide,
    The snow in the street, and the wind on the door,
What hap do you deem there should us betide?
    Minstrels and maids, stand forth on the floor.

"Under a bent when the night was deep,
    The snow in the street, and the wind on the door,
There lay three shepherds, tending their sheep.
    Minstrels and maids, stand forth on the floor."

"O ye shepherds, what have ye seen,
    The snow in the street, and the wind on the door,
To stay your sorrow and heal your teen?"
    "Minstrels and maids, stand forth on the floor.

"In an ox-stall this night we saw,
    The snow in the street, and the wind on the door,
A Babe and a maid without a flaw.
    Minstrels and maids, stand forth on the floor.

"There was an old man there beside;
    The snow in the street, and the wind on the door,
His hair was white, and his hood was wide.
    Minstrels and maids, stand forth on the floor.

"And as we gazed this thing upon,
    The snow in the street, and the wind on the door,
Those twain knelt down to the little one,
    Minstrels and maids stand forth on the floor.

"And a marvellous song we straight did hear,
    The snow in the street, and the wind on the door,
That slew our sorrow and healed our care.
    Minstrels and maids, stand forth on the floor.

"News of a fair and marvellous thing,
    The snow in the street, and the wind on the door,
Nowell, Nowell, Nowell, we sing.
    Minstrels and maids, stand forth on the floor.
        From far away we come to you,
        To tell of great tidings, strange and true."

William Morris

THE SONG OF THE SHEPHERDS

It was near the first cock-crowing,
And Orion's wheel was going,
When an angel stood before us and our hearts were
    sore afraid.
Lo, his face was like the lightning,
When the walls of heaven are whitening,
And he brought us wondrous tidings of a joy that
    shall not fade.

Then a Splendor shone around us,
In a still field where he found us,
A-watch upon the Shepherd Tower and waiting for
    the light;
There where David, as a stripling,
Saw the ewes and lambs go rippling
Down the little hills and hollows at the falling of
    the night.

Oh, what tender, sudden faces
Filled the old familiar places,
The barley-fields where Ruth of old went gleaning
    with the birds!
Down the skies the host came swirling,
Like sea-waters white and whirling,
And our hearts were strangely shaken by the wonder
    of their words.

Haste, O people: all are bidden—
Haste from places, high or hidden:

In Mary's Child the Kingdom comes, the heaven in
    Beauty bends!
He has made all life completer:
He has made the Plain Way sweeter:
For the stall is His first shelter and the cattle His
    first friends.

He has come! the skies are telling:
He has quit the glorious dwelling;
And first the tidings came to us, the humble shepherd
    folk.
He has come to field and manger,
And no more is God a Stranger:
He comes as Common Man at home with cart and
    crookèd yoke.

As a shadow of a cedar
To a traveler in Gray Kedar
Will be the kingdom of His love, the kingdom without
    end.
Tongues and Ages may disclaim Him,
Yet the Heaven of heavens will name Him
Lord of peoples, Light of nations, elder Brother,
    tender Friend.

Edwin Markham

THE SHEPHERD WHO STAYED

There are in Paradise
Souls neither great nor wise,
Yet souls who wear no less
The crown of faithfulness.

My master bade me watch the flock by night;
My duty was to stay. I do not know
What thing my comrades saw in that great light,'
I did not heed the words that bade them go,
I know not were they maddened or afraid;
    I only know I stayed.

The hillside seemed on fire; I felt the sweep
Of wings above my head; I ran to see
If any danger threatened these my sheep.
What though I found them folded quietly,
What though my brother wept and plucked my sleeve,
    They were not mine to leave.

Thieves in the wood and wolves upon the hill,
My duty was to stay. Strange though it may be,
I had no thought to hold my mates, no will
To bid them wait and keep the watch with me.
I had not heard that summons they obeyed;
    I only know I stayed.

Perchance they will return upon the dawn
With word of Bethlehem and why they went.
I only know that watching here alone,
I know a strange content.
I have not failed that trust upon me laid;
    I ask no more—I stayed.

Theodosia Garrison

THE LAME SHEPHERD

Slowly I followed on,
Stumbling and falling.
All the air sparkled;
All the air sung.
Even to my dull heart
Glory was calling;
Slowly I followed on,
Stumbling and falling.

Great wings arched over me,
Purple and amber;
Night was all color,
Night was all gleam.
Wearily up the hill
Needs must I clamber,
Though wings arched over me,
Purple and amber.

Proudly the chorus pealed
While I was panting.
Winds were all music,
Voices all praise;
Brooks, birds, the waving trees
Joined in the chanting;
Proudly the chorus pealed,
While I was panting.

Late came my aching feet,
Late to the manger;

All slept in silence,
All dreamed in dusk;
Under the same dear stars,
No star a stranger,
Late came my aching feet,
Late to the manger.

Kissing a baby's hand,
Painfully kneeling,
Sweet little drowsy hand,
Honey of heaven,
Swift through my twisted limbs
Glowed a glad healing,
Kissing a baby's hand,
Kissing and kneeling.

Katherine Lee Bates

THE FIRST BEST CHRISTMAS NIGHT

Like small curled feathers, white and soft,
  The little clouds went by,
Across the moon, and past the stars,
  And down the western sky:
In upland pasture, where the grass
  With frosted dew was white,
Like snowy clouds the young sheep lay,
  That first, best Christmas night.

The shepherds slept: and glimmering faint,
  With twist of thin, blue smoke,

56487

Only their fire's crackling flames
    The tender silence broke—
Save when a young lamb raised his head,
    Or when the night wind blew,
A nesting bird would softly stir,
    Where dusky olives grew—

With finger on her solemn lip,
    Night hushed the shadowy earth,
And only stars and angels saw
    The little Saviour's birth:
Then came such flash of silver light
    Across the bending skies,
The wondering shepherds woke, and hid
    Their frightened, dazzled eyes.

And all their gentle, sleepy flock
    Looked up, then slept again,
Nor knew the light that dimmed the stars
    Brought endless peace to men—
Nor even heard the gracious words
    That down the ages ring—
"The Christ is born! the Lord has come,
    Good-will on earth to bring!"

Then o'er the moonlit, misty fields,
    Dumb with the world's great joy,
The shepherds sought the white-walled town,
    Where lay the baby boy—

And oh, the gladness of the world,
  The glory of the skies,
Because the longed-for Christ looked up
  In Mary's happy eyes!

Margaret Deland

SONG OF A SHEPHERD BOY AT BETHLEHEM

Sleep, Thou little Child of Mary,
  Rest Thee now.
Though these hands be rough from shearing
  And the plow,
Yet they shall not ever fail Thee,
When the waiting nations hail Thee,
Bringing palms unto their King.
  Now—I sing.

Sleep, Thou little Child of Mary,
  Hope divine.
If Thou wilt but smile upon me,
  I will twine
Blossoms for Thy garlanding.
Thou'rt so little to be King,
  God's Desire!
  Not a brier
Shall be left to grieve Thy brow;
  Rest Thee now.

Sleep, Thou little Child of Mary,
  Some fair day

Wilt Thou, as Thou wert a brother,
  Come away
Over hills and over hollow?
All the lambs will up and follow,
Follow but for love of Thee.
  Lov'st Thou me?

Sleep, Thou little Child of Mary,
  Rest Thee now.
I that watch am come from sheep-stead
  And from plough.
Thou wilt have disdain of me
When Thou'rt lifted, royally,
Very high for all to see:
  Smilest Thou?

Josephine Preston Peabody

THE OTHER SHEPHERD

I was the Other Shepherd—
  I heeded not their cry—
What was one great star the more
  In that deep-studded sky?

I followed not the Messenger—
  How should my soul have known?
It might have been some singing lad,
  His burnous far outblown!

My brothers followed him—
They came back nevermore
Thrifty and wise as they have been,
Counting the fleece and store;

Their eyes were bright with dreams—
They knelt along the sod
And babbled of some stranger-child
They called the Lamb of God;

There was a light across their brows,
A dream behind their eyes
That held their hearts from joy of gain,
Their hands from merchandise.

How could I stop to heed
The tale they had to tell?
I had the flocks to keep and watch
The fleece to pile and sell . . .

Aye, I was very wise
Who followed not their way—
Great are the flocks and herds I own
And wide my lands today—

I wish I could not hear in sleep
The messenger's clear cry,
Or see the flocking cloud-wings
Far off in that deep sky.

I wish I could not hear the voice—
"Thy sorrow—thine the sin.
Thou who wert called by the messenger
And wouldst not enter in!"
                              Margaret Widdemer

I DO NOT LIKE A ROOF TONIGHT

I do not like a roof tonight,
I long to walk a barren field—or lie
Face upward on a hill and watch the sky
Sparkle with silver—and to know
That one night, long ago,
These same stars, with the same hand guiding them,
Shone down on Bethlehem.

A *roof* shuts out the stars—it drugs with sleep,
I wish I were a shepherd of white sheep
Out on the hills, and for their sake
Must keep awake . . .
And I would see the radiance of the sky,
The rapture of the slow stars marching by:
The near ones bright—the far ones very dim.
But speaking, every one, of Him.

I do not like a roof tonight,
But from the fields, if I should hasten down
Toward the glimmering lights of any town,
I think that I should find the Christ-child there
Under a star—somewhere.
Faith or fancy—call it as you will—
The stars at Christmas guide me to Him still.
                              Grace Noll Crowell

V

BEHOLD THERE CAME WISE MEN FROM THE EAST

*The Kings of the East are riding
Tonight to Bethlehem.*

WAITING FOR THE KINGS

Over the frozen plain snow-white
The three Kings will come tonight;
We shall know by the kettle-drums
Which way the procession comes.   .

They have come from very far,
Following fast behind a Star,
In their shimmering robes of silk,
Riding horses white as milk.

They bring thro' the starlit dark
Gold once hid in Noë's Ark;
They bear over snow and ice
Bags of musk and myrrh and spice.

They have brought from the warm countree
Cloves like nails from a blossoming tree,
Flowers of a branch of a Tree that grew
In Eden when the world was new.

They have heard of a wondrous thing,
That here is born a little King;
They bring treasures of great worth
To the Treasure of the earth.

When we see the Kings ride past,
Thro' the silence white and vast,

In the night will bloom, methinks,
Velvet roses and striped pinks.

When we see them all aglow
Riding over leagues of snow,
In their robes of red and gold,
We shall never feel the cold.

We shall print upon the gifts
They have borne through the snow-drifts,
Thro' the bitter weather wild,
Kisses for the little Child.

R. L. Gales

THE THREE KINGS

Three Kings came riding from far away,
    Melchior and Gaspar and Balthasar;
Three Wise Men out of the East were they,
And they travelled by night and they slept by day,
    For their guide was a beautiful, wonderful star.

The star was so beautiful, large and clear,
    That all the other stars of the sky
Became a white mist in the atmosphere,
And by this they knew that the coming was near
    Of the Prince foretold in the prophecy.

Three caskets they bore on their saddle-bows,
    Three caskets of gold with golden keys;

Their robes were of crimson silk with rows
Of bells and pomegranates and furbelows,
  Their turbans like blossoming almond-trees.

And so the Three Kings rode into the West,
  Through the dusk of night, over hill and dell,
And sometimes they nodded with beard on breast,
And sometimes talked, as they paused to rest,
  With the people they met at some wayside well.

"Of the Child that is born," said Balthasar,
  "Good people, I pray you, tell us the news;
For we in the East have seen His star,
And have ridden fast, and have ridden far,
  To find and worship the King of the Jews."

And the people answered, "You ask in vain;
  We know of no king but Herod the Great!"
They thought the Wise Men were men insane,
As they spurred their horses across the plain,
  Like riders in haste, and who cannot wait.

And when they came to Jerusalem,
  Herod the Great, who had heard this thing,
Sent for the Wise Men and questioned them;
And said, "Go down unto Bethlehem,
  And bring me tidings of this new King."

So they rode away and the star stood still,
  The only one in the gray of morn;

Yes, it stopped,—it stood still of its own free will,
Right over Bethlehem on the hill,
   The city of David, where Christ was born.

And the Three Kings rode through the gate and the
     guard,
   Through the silent street, till their horses turned
And neighed as they entered the great inn-yard;
But the windows were closed, and the doors were
     barred,
   And only a light in the stable burned.

And cradled there in the scented hay,
   In the air made sweet by the breath of kine,
The little Child in the manger lay,
The Child, that would be King one day
   Of a kingdom not human but divine.

His mother, Mary of Nazareth
   Sat watching beside His place of rest,
Watching the even flow of His breath,
For the joy of life and the terror of death
   Were mingled together in her breast.

They laid their offerings at His feet:
   The gold was their tribute to a King,
The frankincense, with its odor sweet,
Was for the Priest, the Paraclete,
   The myrrh for the body's burying.

And the mother wondered and bowed her head,
   And sat as still as a statue of stone;

Her heart was troubled yet comforted,
Remembering what the Angel had said
    Of an endless reign and of David's throne.

Then the Kings rode out of the city gate,
    With a clatter of hoofs in proud array;
But they went not back to Herod the Great,
For they knew his malice and feared his hate,
    And returned to their homes by another way.
                            Henry Wadsworth Longfellow

THE KINGS OF THE EAST

The Kings of the East are riding
    Tonight to Bethlehem.
The sunset glows dividing,
The Kings of the East are riding;
A star their journey guiding,
    Gleaming with gold and gem
The Kings of the East are riding
    Tonight to Bethlehem.

To a strange sweet harp of Zion
    The starry host troops forth;
The golden-glaived Orion
To a strange sweet harp of Zion;
The Archer and the Lion,
    The Watcher of the North;
To a strange sweet harp of Zion
    The starry host sweeps forth.

There beams above a manger
  The child-face of a star;
Amid the stars a stranger,
It beams above a manger;
What means this ether-ranger
  To pause where poor folk are?
There beams above a manger
  The child-face of a star.

Katherine Lee Bates

A BALLAD OF WISE MEN

When that our gentle Lord was born
  And cradled in the hay,
There rode three wise men from the east,—
  Three rich wise men were they;
All in the starry night they came
  Their homage gifts to pay.

They got them down from camel-back
  The cattle shed before,
And in the darkness vainly sought
  A great latch on the door,
"Ho, this is strange!" quoth Balthazar.
  "Aye, strange!" quoth Melchior.

Quoth Gaspar, "I can find no hasp;
  Well hidden is the lock";
"The door," quoth Melchior, "is stout
  And fast, our skill to mock";
Quoth Balthazar, "The little King
  Might wake, we dare not knock."

The three wise men they sat them down
    To wait for morning dawn,
The cunning wards of that old door
    They thought and marvelled on;
Quoth they, "No gate in all the East
    Hath bar-bolts tighter drawn."

Anon there came a little lad
    With lambskins for the King;
He had no key, he raised no latch,
    He touched no hidden spring,
But gently pushed the silent door
    And open it gan swing.

"A miracle! a miracle!"
    Cried out the wise men three;
"A little child hath solved the locks
    That could not opened be."
In wonder spake the shepherd lad,
    "It hath no locks," quoth he.

                    George M. P. Baird

THE THREE KINGS OF COLOGNE

From out Cologne there came three kings
    To worship Jesus Christ, their King.
To Him they sought, fine herbs they brought,
    And many a beauteous golden thing;
    They brought their gifts to Bethlehem town,
And in that manger set them down.

Then spake the first king, and he said:
  "O Child, most heavenly, bright, and fair!
I bring this crown to Bethlehem town
  For Thee, and only Thee, to wear;
  So give a heavenly crown to me
When I shall come at last to Thee!"

The second, then. "I bring Thee here
  This royal robe, O Child!" he cried;
"Of silk 'tis spun, and such an one
  There is not in the world beside;
  So in the day of doom requite
Me with a heavenly robe of white."

The third king gave his gift, and quoth:
  "Spikenard and myrrh to Thee I bring,
And with these twain would I most fain
  Anoint the body of my King;
  So may their incense sometime rise
To plead for me in yonder skies!"

Thus spake the three kings of Cologne,
  That gave their gifts and went away;
And now kneel I in prayer hard by
  The cradle of the Child today;
  Nor crown, nor robe, nor spice I bring
As offering unto Christ, my King.

Yet have I brought a gift the Child
  May not despise, however small;
For here I lay my heart today,

And it is full of love for all.
Take Thou the poor but loyal thing,
My only tribute, Christ, my king!
Eugene Field

BABUSHKA

Babushka sits before the fire
  Upon a winter's night;
The driving winds heap up the snow,
  Her hut is snug and tight;
The howling winds,—they only make
  Babushka's fire more bright!

She hears a knocking at the door:
  So late—who can it be?
She hastes to lift the wooden latch,
  No thought of fear has she;
The wind-blown candle in her hand
  Shines out on strangers three.

Their beards are white with age, and snow
  That in the darkness flies;
Their floating locks are long and white,
  But kindly are their eyes
That sparkle underneath their brows,
  Like stars in frosty skies.

"Babushka, we have come from far,
  We tarry but to say,

A little Prince is born this night,
   Who all the world shall sway.
Come join the search, come, go with us,
   Who go our gifts to pay."

Babushka shivers at the door;
   "I would I might behold
The little Prince who shall be King
   But ah! the night is cold,
The wind so fierce, the snow so deep,
   And I, good sirs, am old."

The strangers three, no word they speak,
   But fade in snowy space!
Babushka sits before her fire,
   And dreams, with wistful face:
"I would that I had questioned them,
   So I the way might trace!

"When morning comes with blessèd light;
   I'll early be awake:
My staff in hand I'll go,—perchance,
   Those strangers I'll o'ertake;
And, for the Child some little toys
   I'll carry, for His sake."

The morning came, and staff in hand,
   She wandered in the snow,
She asked the way of all she met,
   But none the way could show.
"It must be farther yet," she sighed:
   "Then farther will I go."

And still, 'tis said, on Christmas Eve,
   When high the drifts are piled,
With staff, with basket on her arm,
   Babushka seeks the Child:
At every door her face is seen,—
   Her wistful face and mild!

Her gifts at every door she leaves:
   She bends and murmurs low,
Above each little face half-hid
   By pillows white as snow:
"And is He here?" Then, softly sighs,
   "Nay, farther must I go!"

                    Edith M. Thomas

A CHRISTMAS CAROL

The kings, they came from the south,
   All dressed in ermine fine,
They bore Him gold and chrysoprase,
   And gifts of precious wine.

The shepherds came from out the north,
   Their coats were brown and old;
They brought Him little new-born lambs—
   They had not any gold.

The wise men came from out the east,
   And they were wrapped in white;
The star that led them all the way,
   Did glorify the night.

The angels came from Heaven high,
   And they were clad with wings,
And lo! they brought a joyful song
   The host of heaven sings.

The kings they knocked upon the door;
   The shepherds entered in;
The wise men followed after them,
   To hear the song begin.

The angels sang throughout the night,
   Until the rising sun,
But little Jesus fell asleep
   Before the song was done.

Sara Teasdale

OH, BRING NOT GOLD!

Oh, bring not gold this Christmas night!
   'Twas gold that Gaspar bore.
And bring not frankincense such as
   Was borne by Melchior:
Nor myrrh whose dusky breath perfumed
   Slim hands of Balthasar!
No: bring not these, the gifts of earth,
   However rich you are!

What has a Child to do with gold
   And greedy bartering;
And what to do with frankincense
   And stilted worshipping?

What has a Child to do with myrrh
　　And tombs, death-staled and dim?
Nay, have you coffers, crowns, rich robes,
　　Bring not these gifts to Him!

But come to Him this Christmas night
　　As once the shepherds came,
With empty hands, yet, in their eyes,
　　Burned wonder's subtle flame,
And in their minds was quiet faith,
　　And in their hearts the tall
White flower of love. Such gifts they bore
　　Who bore no gifts at all.

Now, in your eyes, let wonder be;
　　Let love be in your heart;
Faith in your mind, unworldly things
　　Not sold in any mart—
And yet, a Child had need of these.
　　Who bear such gifts, draw nigh!
For these give peace not frankincense
　　Nor myrrh nor gold can buy.
　　　　　　　　　Violet Alleyn Storey

A SONG FOR THE SEASON

The Kings to the Stable
They brought sweet spice,
The gold and the silver,
And jewels of price.

But the Dove by the manger
She would not cease
Mourning so softly:
Bring Him Peace! Bring Him Peace!
The Kings from the Orient
Brought nard and clove.
The Dove went mourning:
Bring Him Love; bring Him Love.
What would content Him
In silver and gold,—
A new-born Baby
But one hour old?
Not myrrh shall please Him
Nor the ambergris.
What hath sweet savour
Of His mother's kiss?
There is clash of battle,
And men hate and slay:
From the noise and tumult
She hides Him away.
But His sleep is fitful
In His mother's breast,
The Dove goes mourning:
Give Him rest; give Him rest!

Katharine Tynan

VI

THE BIRDS PRAISE HIM

Some say that ever 'gainst that season comes
Wherein our Savior's birth is celebrated,
The Bird of Dawning singeth all night long.

CAROL OF THE BIRDS

Whence comes this rush of wings afar,
Following straight the Noël star?
Birds from the woods in wondrous flight,
Bethlehem seek this Holy Night.

"Tell us, ye birds, why come ye here,
Into this stable, poor and drear?"
"Hast'ning we seek the new-born King,
And all our sweetest music bring."

Hark how the green-finch bears his part,
Philomel, too, with tender heart,
Chants from her leafy dark retreat
Re, mi, fa, sol, in accents sweet.

Angels and shepherds, birds of the sky,
Come where the Son of God doth lie;
Christ on the earth with man doth dwell,
Join in the shout, Noël, Noël.

Bas-Quercy

THE BIRDS PRAISE THE ADVENT OF THE SAVIOUR

When in the Eastern skies the wondrous Star did rise
    And fill the night with splendour,
Came birds in joyful throng to sound their dainty song
    In a carol sweet and tender.

Hosanna to the Child and His mother mild
  Full reverently to render.
The kingly eagle came to praise His holy name
  In mighty proclamation,
The sparrow then replied, "Tonight is Christmas-tide,
  A night of jubilation."
Then robin red-breast sang: "Now death has lost its
     pang,
  In Christ is our salvation."
The nightingale sang sweet the Holy Babe to greet,
  In Mary's arms a-lying,
The cuckoo and the quail flew over hill and dale
  In admiration vying,
The barn-owl's eyes were dim, such radiance blinded
     him,
    And homeward he went flying.
Spanish Carol of the XV Century

THE LEAST OF CAROLS

Loveliest dawn of gold and rose
Steals across undrifted snows;
In brown, rustling oak leaves stir
Squirrel, nuthatch, woodpecker;
Brief their matins, but by noon.
All the sunny wood's a-tune:
Jays, forgetting their harsh cries,
Pipe a spring note, clear and true;
Wheel on angel wings of blue,

Trumpeters of Paradise;
Then the tiniest feathered thing,
All a-flutter, tail and wing,
Gives himself to caroling:

"Chick-a-dee-dee, chick-a-dee!
Jesulino, hail to thee!
Lowliest baby born today,
Pillowed on a wisp of hay;
King no less of sky and earth.
    And singing sea;
Jesu! Jesu! most and least!
For the sweetness of thy birth
Every little bird and beast,
Wind and wave and forest tree,
Praises God exceedingly,
    Exceedingly."

Sophie Jewett

THE CHRISTMAS SILENCE

Hushed are the pigeons cooing low
    On dusty rafters of the loft;
    And mild-eyed oxen, breathing soft,
Sleep on the fragrant hay below.

Dim shadows in the corner hide;
    The glimmering lantern's rays are shed
    Where one small lamb just lifts his head,
Then huddles 'gainst his mother's side.

Strange silence tingles in the air;
   Through the half-open door a bar
   Of light from one low-hanging star
Touches a baby's radiant hair.

No sound: the mother, kneeling, lays
   Her cheek against the little face.
   Oh human love! Oh heavenly grace!
'Tis yet in silence that she prays!

Ages of silence end to-night;
   Then to the long-expectant earth
   Glad angels come to greet His birth
In burst of music, love, and light!

                    Margaret Deland

FIRST CHRISTMAS NIGHT OF ALL

That first Christmas night of all,
No lights were in the dreaming town,
No steeples shook their tidings down,
   No carols raised their call.

But music broke upon a hill,
And all the dark was strangely stirred
With beauty of bright angel's word—
   A word that echoes still.

And in a dim and dusty stall
A little light began to glow,

That Christmas night so long ago—
First Christmas night of all!
Nancy Byrd Turner

BEFORE THE PALING OF THE STARS

Before the paling of the stars,
    Before the winter morn,
Before the earliest cockcrow,
    Jesus Christ was born:
Born in a stable,
    Cradled in a manger,
In the world His hands had made
    Born a stranger.

Priest and King lay fast asleep
    In Jerusalem,
Young and old lay fast asleep
    In crowded Bethlehem:
Saint and Angel, ox and ass,
    Kept a watch together
Before the Christmas daybreak
    In the winter weather.

Jesus on His Mother's breast
    In the stable cold,
Spotless Lamb of God was He,
    Shepherd of the fold:
Let us kneel with Mary Maid,
    With Joseph bent and hoary,

With Saint and Angel, ox and ass,
To hail the King of Glory.
Christina Rossetti

HIS BIRTHDAY

The day the Christ-child's tender eyes
    Unveiled their beauty on the earth,
God lit a new star in the skies
    To flash the message of His birth;
And wise men read the glowing sign,
And came to greet the Child divine.

Low kneeling in the stable's gloom,
    Their precious treasure they unrolled:
The place was rich with sweet perfume;
    Upon the floor lay gifts of gold.
And thus adoring they did bring
To Christ the earliest offering.

I think no nimbus wreathed the head
    Of the young King so rudely throned;
The quilt of hay beneath Him spread
    The sleepy kine beside Him owned;
And here and there in the torn thatch
The sky thrust in a starry patch.

Oh, when was new-born monarch shrined
    Within such canopy as this?

The birds have cradles feather lined;
   And for their new babes princesses
Have sheets of lace without a flaw,—
   His pillow was a wisp of straw!

He chose this way, it may have been,
   That those poor mothers, everywhere,
Whose babies in the world's great inn
   Find scanty cradle-room and fare,
As did the Babe of Bethlehem,
So find somewhat to comfort them.

May Riley Smith

CHRISTMAS

There is a silence
On the listening earth . . .
Royal folk and humble
Wait the King's birth.
Snow in the meadow—
Snow in the mart—
But all the songs of Christmas
Sing through my heart!

There is a darkness
Across the world tonight . . .
But oh, the still glory
Of one star's light!
Dear star of Christmas,
Shine softly when
In the blessèd manger
He is born again!

So may the holy
Angel-voices sing! . . .
So may the star shine
For the little King! . . .
So may we, as pilgrims,
Seek where He lies . . .
All the love of Christmas
Is in His eyes!

Catherine Parmenter

A CHRISTMAS CAROL

In the bleak mid-winter
    Frosty wind made moan,
Earth stood hard as iron,
    Water like a stone;
Snow had fallen, snow on snow,
    Snow on snow,
In the bleak mid-winter
    Long ago.

Our God, Heaven cannot hold Him
    Nor earth sustain;
Heaven and earth shall flee away
    When He comes to reign.
In the bleak mid-winter
    A stable-place sufficed
The Lord God Almighty
    Jesus Christ.

Angels and archangels
  May have gathered there,
Cherubim and seraphim
  Thronged the air;
But only His Mother
  In her maiden bliss
Worshipped her Belovèd
  With a kiss.

What can I give Him,
  Poor as I am?
If I were a shepherd
  I would bring a lamb,
If I were a Wise Man,
  I would do my part,—
Yet what I can I give Him,
  Give my heart.

Christina Rossetti

CAROL

When the herds were watching
  In the midnight chill,
Came a spotless lambkin
  From the heavenly hill.

Snow was on the mountains,
  And the wind was cold,
When from God's own garden
  Dropped a rose of gold.

When 'twas bitter winter,
  Houseless and forlorn
In a star-lit stable
  Christ the Babe was born.

Welcome, heavenly Lambkin;
  Welcome, golden Rose;
Alleluia, Baby,
  In the swaddling clothes!

William Canton

UNTO US A SON IS GIVEN

Given, not lent,
But not withdrawn—once sent,
This Infant of mankind, this One,
Is still the little welcome Son.

New every year,
New-born and newly dear,
He comes with tidings and a song,
The ages long, the ages long.

Even as the cold
Keen winter grows not old
As childhood is so fresh, foreseen,
And spring in the familiar green.

Sudden as sweet
Come the expected feet,

All joy is young, and new all art,
And He, too, whom we have by heart.
Alice Meynell

THE NEIGHBORS OF BETHLEHEM

Good neighbor, tell me why that sound,
That noisy tumult rising round,
Awaking all in slumber lying?
Truly disturbing are these cries,
All through the quiet village flying,
O come ye shepherds, wake, arise!

What, neighbor, then do ye not know
God hath appeared on earth below
And now is born in manger lowly!
In humble guise He came this night,
Simple and meek, this Infant holy,
Yet how divine in beauty bright.

Good neighbor, I must make amend,
Forthwith to bring Him will I send,
And Joseph with the gentle Mother.
When to my home these three I bring,
Then will it far outshine all other,
A palace fair for greatest king!
French Carol of the 13th Century

A COUNTRY CAROL

Where the patient oxen were, by the ass's stall,
Watching my Lord's manger knelt the waking cattle
all;
'Twas a little country maid vigil by him kept—
All among the country things my good Lord slept.
Fair was Rome the city on that early Christmas morn,
Yet among the country-folk was my Lord born!

Country-lads that followed Him, blithe they were and
kind,
It was only city-folk were hard to Him and blind:
Ay, He told of lilies, and of grain and grass that grew,
Fair things of the summer fields my good Lord knew,
By the hedgerows' flowering there He laid His head—
It was in the country that my Lord was bred.

When the cross weighed down on him, on the grievous
road,
'Twas a kindly countryman raised my good Lord's
load;
Peasant girls of Galilee, folk of Nazareth,
These were fain to follow Him down the ways of
death—
Yea, beyond a city wall, underneath the sky,
Out in open country did my good Lord die.

When He rose to Heaven on that white Ascension day
Last from open country did my good Lord pass away;

Rows of golden seraphim watched where He should
    dwell,
Yet it was the country-folk had my Lord's farewell:
Out above the flowered hill, from the mossy grass,
Up from open country did my good Lord pass.

Where the jeweled minsters are, where the censers
    sway,
There they kneel to Christ the Lord on this His
    bearing-day:
But I shall stay to greet Him where the bonny fields
    begin,
Like the fields that once my good Lord wandered in,
Where His thorn-tree flowered once, where His sparrows
    soared,
In the open country-land of my good Lord.

Margaret Widdemer

CAROL

Mary, the mother, sits on the hill,
And cradles Child Jesu, that lies so still;
She cradles Child Jesu, that sleeps so sound,
And the little wind blows the song around.

The little wind blows the mother's words,
"Ei, Jesu, ei," like the song of birds;
"Ei, Jesu, ei," I heard it still,
As I lay asleep at the foot of the hill.

"Sleep, Babe, sleep, mother watch doth keep,
Ox shall not hurt Thee, nor ass, nor sheep;

Dew falls sweet from Thy Father's sky,
Sleep, Jesu, sleep; ei, Jesu ei."

Langdon E. Mitchell

THE MADONNA OF THE CARPENTER SHOP

O Mary, in thy clear young eyes
   What sorrow came at His first cry?
   What hint of how He was to die
Disturbed thee in the calm sunrise . . .
   What shadow from the paling sky
Did fall across thy Paradise?

Dreamd'st thou the Garden, and the Tree?
   Know they were for the little Child
   Whose lips against thy warm breast smiled?
So sweet, that body close to thee,
   By men's rough hands to be defiled;
So frail . . . yet waiting Calvary!

Ruth Guthrie Harding

JOYS SEVEN

The first good joy that Mary had,
   It was the joy of one;
To see the blessèd Jesus Christ
   When He was first her son:

   When He was first her son, good man:
     And blessèd may He be,
   Both Father, Son, and Holy Ghost,
     To all eternity.

The next good joy that Mary had,
   It was the joy of two;
To see her own son, Jesus Christ,
   To make the lame to go:

The next good joy that Mary had,
   It was the joy of three;
To see her own son, Jesus Christ,
   To make the blind to see:

The next good joy that Mary had,
   It was the joy of four;
To see her own son, Jesus Christ,
   To read the Bible o'er:

The next good joy that Mary had,
   It was the joy of five;
To see her own son, Jesus Christ,
   To bring the dead alive:

The next good joy that Mary had,
   It was the joy of six;
To see her own son, Jesus Christ,
   Upon the crucifix:

The next good joy that Mary had,
   It was the joy of seven;
To see her own son, Jesus Christ,
   To wear the crown of heaven.

                         Old Carol

VII

THE TREES PRAISE HIM

*For this is the Tree whose blessed yield
Bears seed in darkest ground.*

THE HOLLY AND THE IVY

The Holly and the Ivy,
  Now both are full well grown:
Of all the trees that spring in wood,
  The Holly bears the crown.
The Holly bears a blossom,
  As white as lily flow'r;
And Mary bore sweet Jesus Christ.
  To be our sweet Saviour;
  TO BE OUR SWEET SAVIOUR.

The Holly bears a berry.
  As red as any blood;
And Mary bore sweet Jesus Christ,
  To do poor sinners good.
The holly bears a prickle,
  As sharp as any thorn;
And Mary bore sweet Jesus Christ,
  On Christmas day in the morn,
  ON CHRISTMAS DAY IN THE MORN.

The holly bears a bark,
  As bitter as any gall:
And Mary bore sweet Jesus Christ,
  For to redeem us all.
The Holly and the Ivy,
  Now both are full well grown;

Of all the trees that spring in wood,
The Holly bears the crown,
THE HOLLY BEARS THE CROWN.
Old English Song

HOLLY CAROL

Toward the doors of lonely folk
   And such as wait in dread
The Christ-child comes to us
   With holly round His head.

Light He brings and laughter
   And a bright holly wreath
To show them how the thorn-leaves
   Have scarlet fruit beneath.

And where there is happiness
   And none who need mourn
He stands on their pathways
   With His wreath of thorn;

He stands in their doorways
   Where joy is in the air
With holly for a prick to those
   Who have joy to share—

He comes to men's hearthstones,
   Telling all of them
How that joy and sorrow
   Flourish on one stem;

The holly is a bright promise
  That hearts need not break,
The holly is a gift to us
  To keep joy awake;

Early Christmas morning
  When first dawn is shed
The Christ-child comes to us
  With holly round His head.
                    Margaret Widdemer

CHRISTMAS EVE

In holly hedges starving birds
  Silently mourn the setting year;
Upright like silver-plated swords
  The flags stand in the frozen mere.

The mistletoe we still adore
  Upon the twisted hawthorn grows:
In antique gardens hellebore
  Puts forth its blushing Christmas rose.

Shrivell'd and purple, cheek by jowl,
  The hips and haws hang drearily;
Roll'd in a ball the sulky owl
  Creeps far into his hollow tree.

In abbeys and cathedrals dim
  The birth of Christ is acted o'er;

The kings of Cologne worship him,
   Balthazar, Jasper, Melchior.

The shepherds in the field at night
   Beheld an angel glory-clad,
And shrank away with sore afright.
   "Be not afraid," the angel bade.

"I bring good news to king and clown,
   To you here crouching on the sward;
For there is born in David's town
   A Saviour, which is Christ the Lord.

"Behold the babe is swathed, and laid
   Within a manger." Straight there stood
Beside the angel all arrayed
   A heavenly multitude.

"Glory to God," they sang; "and peace,
   Good pleasure among men."
The wondrous message of release!
   Glory to God again!

Hush! Hark! the waits, far up the street!
   A distant, ghostly charm unfolds!
Of magic music, wild and sweet,
   Anemones and clarigolds.

John Davidson

SIX GREEN SINGERS

The frost of the moon stood over my floor
And six green singers stood at my door.

"What do ye here that music make?"
"Let us come in for Christ's sweet Sake."

"Long have ye journeyed in coming here?"
"Our Pilgrimage was the length of the year."

"Where do ye make for?" I asked of them.
"Our Shrine is a Stable in Bethlehem."

"What will ye do as ye go along?"
"Sing to the world an ever-green song."

"What will ye sing for the listening earth?"
"One will sing of a brave-souled Mirth,

"One of the Holiest Mystery,
The Glory of Glories shall one song be,

"One of the Memory of things,
One of the Child's imaginings,

"One of our songs is the fadeless Faith,
And all are of Life more mighty than death."

"Ere ye be gone that music make,
Give me an alms for Christ's sweet Sake."

"Six green branches we leave with you;
See they be scattered your house-place through.

"The staunch blithe Holly your board shall grace,
Mistletoe bless your chimney-place,

"Laurel to crown your lighted hall,
Over your bed let the Yew-bough fall,

"Close by the cradle the Christmas Fir,
For elfin dreams in its branches stir,

"Last and loveliest, high and low,
From ceil to floor let the Ivy go."

From each glad guest I received my gift
And then the latch of the door did lift—

"Green singers, God prosper the song ye make
As ye sing to the world for Christ's sweet Sake."

                                        Eleanor Farjeon

THE CAROL OF THE FIR TREE

Quoth the Fir-tree, 'Orange and vine'
    Sing 'Nowell, Nowell, Nowell'!
'Have their honour: I have mine!'
    In Excelsis Gloria!
'I am kin to the great king's house,'
    Ring 'Nowell, Nowell, Nowell'!

'And Lebanon whispers in my boughs.'
In Excelsis Gloria!

'Apple and cherry, pear and plum,'
  Winds of Autumn, sigh 'Nowell'!
'All the trees like magis come'
  Bending low with 'Gloria'!
'Holding out on every hand'
  Summer pilgrims to Nowell!
'Gorgeous gifts from Elfin-land.'
  And the May saith 'Gloria'!

'Out of the darkness—who shall say'
  Gold and myrrh for this Nowell:
'How they win their wizard way?'
  Out of the East with 'Gloria'!
'Men that eat of the sun and dew'
  Angels laugh and sing, 'Nowell'!
'Call it "fruit," and say it "grew"!'
  Into the West with 'Gloria'!

'Leaves that fall,' whispered the fir
  Through the forest sing 'Nowell'!
'I am winter's minister,'
  In Excelsis Gloria!
'Summer friends may come and go,'
  Up the mountain sing 'Nowell'!
'Love abides thro' storm and snow,'
  Down the valley, 'Gloria'!

'Lay the axe at my young stem now!'
  Woodman, woodman! sing 'Nowell'!

'Set a star on every bough!'
In Excelsis Gloria!
'Hall and cot shall see me stand,'
Rich and poor man, sing 'Nowell'!
'Giver of gifts from Elfin-land.'
Oberon, answer 'Gloria'!

'On my boughs, on mine, on mine,'
Father and mother, sing 'Nowell'!
'All the fruits of the earth shall twine.'
Bending low with 'Gloria'!
'Sword of wood and doll of wax'
Little children, sing 'Nowell'!
'Swing on the stem was cleft with an axe!'
Craftsmen all, a 'Gloria'!

'Hear! I have looked on the other side,'
Out of the East, O sing 'Nowell'!
'Because to live this night I died!'
Into the West with 'Gloria'!
'Hear! In this lighted room I have found'
Ye that seek, O sing 'Nowell'!
'The spell that worketh underground.'
Ye that doubt a 'Gloria'!

'I have found it, even I.'
Ye that are lowly, sing 'Nowell'!
'The secret of this alchemy!'
Ye that are poor, a 'Gloria'!

'Look, your tinsel turneth to gold,'
  Sing 'Nowell! Nowell! Nowell'!
'Your dust to a hand for love to hold!'
  In Excelsis Gloria.

'Hung by the hilt on your Christmas-tree'
  Little children, sing 'Nowell'!
'Your wooden sword is a cross for me.'
  Emperors, a 'Gloria'!
'I have found that fabulous stone'
  Ocean worthies, cry 'Nowell'!
'Which turneth all things into one.'
  Wise men all, a Gloria!

'It is not ruby nor anything'
  Jeweller, jeweller, sing 'Nowell'!
'Fit for the crown of an earthly king':
  In Excelsis Gloria.
'It is not here, it is not there!'
  Traveller, rest and cry 'Nowell'!
'It is one thing and everywhere!'
  Heaven and earth sing 'Gloria'!

'It is the earth, the moon, the sun,'
  Mote in the sunbeam, sing 'Nowell'!
'And all the stars that march as one,'
  In Excelsis Gloria!
'Here by the touch of it, I can see'
  Sing, O Life, a sweet Nowell!
'The world's King die on a Christmas-tree,'
  Answer, Death, with a 'Gloria'!

'Here, not set in a realm apart,'
  East and west are one 'Nowell'!
'Holy Land is in your heart!'
  North and South one 'Gloria'!
'Death is a birth, birth is a death,'
  Love is all, O sing 'Nowell'!
'And London one with Nazareth,'
  And all the World a 'Gloria'!

'And angels over your heart's roof sing'
  Birds of God, O pour 'Nowell'!
'That a poor man's son is the Son of a King!'
  Out of your heart this 'Gloria'!
'Round the world you'll not away'
  In your own soul, they sing 'Nowell'!
'From Holy Land this Christmas Day!'
  In your own soul, this 'Gloria'!

                                Alfred Noyes

CHRISTMAS TREES

I saw along each noisy city street
The trees for Christmas, standing dark and still,
The pines and firs come down from field and hill,
Old trees and young that had known sun and sleet.

Soft needles fell on hard, dull pavement there,
And forest rose in a most treeless place;
And there was gladness in each passing face,
And there was balsam fragrance everywhere.

O, Lovely way to celebrate Your Birth
Whose Birth Star glistened through Judea's trees;
Whom Joseph taught the skilful use of these;
Who, on a Tree, once overcame the earth!

Grant then Your blessing, Friend of Trees, we pray,
On those who deck green boughs for Christmas Day!
                                        Violet Alleyn Storey

THE HAUGHTY ASPEN

As I went through the tangled wood
*   I heard the Aspen shiver.*
"What dost thou ail? Sweet Aspen? Say?
Why do thy leaflets quiver?"

" 'Twas long ago," the Aspen sighed—
    How long is past my knowing—
"When Mother Mary rode adown
    This wood where I was growing.
Blest Joseph journey'd by her side,
    Upon his good staff resting,
And in her arms the Heav'nly Babe,
    Dove of the World, was nesting.
Fair was the mother, shining-fair,
    A lily sweetly blowing;
The Babe was but a lily-bud,
    Like to His mothe. showing.

The birds began, 'Thy Master comes!
  Bow down, bow down before Him!
The date, the fig, the hazel tree,
  In rev'rence bent to adore Him.
I only, out of all the host
  Of bird and tree and flower,—
I, haughty, would not bend my head,
  Nor own my Master's power.
'Proud Aspen,' quoth the Mother-Maid,
  'Thy Lord, dost thou defy Him?
When emperors worship at His shrine,
  Wilt courtesy deny Him?'
I heard her voice; my heart was rent,
  My boughs began to shiver,
And age on age, in punishment,
  My sorrowing leaflets quiver."

Still in the dark and tangled wood,
  Still doth the Aspen quiver.
The haughty tree doth bear a curse,
  Her leaflets aye must shiver.
                    Nora Archibald Smith

YULE-TIDE FIRES

Cleanse with the burning log of oak
The canker of thy care,
Deck with the scarlet-berried bough
The temple of the fair;
Spread pure-white linen for a feast,
Perchance some guest may share.

Give forth thy gold and silver coins,
For they were lent to thee;
Put out to usury thy dross,
One talent gaineth three;
Perchance the hungered and the poor
May pray to God for thee.

Once a pale star rose in the East,
For watching herds to see,
And weakness came to Bethlehem
And strength to Galilee.
Perchance! if thou dost keep thy tryst,
A star may rise for thee.

Anonymous

VIII

THE CHRISTMAS FEAST

Make we merry both more and less
For now is the time of Christmas.

LORDLINGS, LISTEN TO OUR LAY

Lordlings, listen to our lay—
We have come from far away
  To seek Christmas;
In this mansion we are told
He his yearly feast doth hold:
    'Tis today!
May joy come from God above,
To all those who Christmas love.

Old Carol

BEGGAR'S RHYME

Christmas is coming, the geese are getting fat,
Please to put a penny in the old man's hat;
If you haven't got a penny, a ha'penny will do,
If you haven't got a ha'penny, God bless you.

From the Old English

THRICE WELCOME CHRISTMAS

Now thrice welcome Christmas,
  Which brings us good cheer,
Minced pies and plum-porridge,
  Good ale and strong beer;

With pig, goose, and capon,
      The best that can be,
So well doth the weather
      And our stomachs agree.

Observe how the chimneys
      Do smoke all about,
The cooks are providing
      For dinner no doubt;
But those on whose tables
      No victuals appear,
O may they keep Lent
      All the rest of the year!

With holly and ivy
      So green and so gay,
We deck up our houses
      As fresh as the day,
With bays and rosemary,
      And laurel complete,
And everyone now
      Is a king in conceit.
            Poor Richard's Almanac, 1695

NOW THAT THE TIME IS COME WHEREIN

Now that the time has come wherein
      Our Saviour Christ was born,
The larders full of beef and pork,
      The garners filled with corn:

As God hath plenty to thee sent,
 Take comfort of thy labours,
And let it never thee repent
 To feast thy needy neighbours.

Let fires in every chimney be
 That people they may warm them:
Tables with dishes covered,
 Good victuals will not harm them.
With mutton, veal, beef, pig and pork,
 Well furnish every board;
Plum-pudding, furmity and what
 Thy stock will them afford.
No niggard of thy liquor be,
 Let it go round thy table;
People may freely drink, but not
 So long as they are able.

Good customs they may be abused,
 Which makes rich men to slack us;
This feast is to relieve the poor
 And not to drunken Bacchus.

Thus if thou doest
 'Twill credit raise thee;
God will thee bless
 And neighbours praise thee.
     Poor Robin's Almanac, 1700

CAROL, BROTHERS, CAROL

Carol, brothers, carol,
  Carol joyfully;
Carol the glad tidings,
  Carol merrily;
And pray a gladsome Christmas
  For all good Christian men.
Carol, brothers, carol,
  Christmas comes again.

Carol ye with gladness,
  Not in songs of earth;
On the Saviour's birthday,
  Hallowed be our mirth.
While a thousand blessings
  Fill our hearts with glee,
Christmas-day we'll keep, the
  Feast of Charity!

At the joyous table,
  Think of those who've none,—
The orphan and the widow,
  Hungry and alone.
Bountiful your offerings,
  To the altar bring;
Let the poor and needy
  Christmas carols sing.

Listening angel-music,
  Discord sure must cease;

Who dare hate his brother,
   On this day of peace?
While the heavens are telling
   To mankind good-will,
Only love and kindness,
   Every bosom fill.

Let our hearts, responding
   To the seraph band,
Wish this morning's sunshine
   Bright in every land!
Word and deed and prayer
   Speed the grateful sound,
Bidding Merry Christmas
   All the world around.
                    Rev. Wm. A. Muhlenberg, D. D.

THE SINGERS IN THE SNOW

God bless the master of this house
   And all that are therein,
And to begin the Christmas tide
   With mirth now let us sing.

   Chorus: For the Saviour of all the people
                Upon this time was born,
                Who did from death deliver us,
                When we were left forlorn.

Then let us all most merry be,
  And sing with cheerful voice,
For we have good occasion now
  This time for to rejoice.

Then put away contention all
  And fall no more at strife,
Let every man with cheerfulness
  Embrace his loving wife.

With plenteous food your houses store,
  Provide some wholesome cheer,
And call your friends together,
  That live both far and near.

Then let us all most merry be,
  Since that we are come here,
And we do hope before we part
  To taste some of your beer.

Your beer, your beer, your Christmas beer,
  That seems to be so strong;
And we do wish that Christmas tide
  Was twenty times as long.

Then sing with voices cheerfully,
  For Christ this time was born,
Who did from death deliver us,
  When we were left forlorn.

                  Old English Carol

HERE WE COME A-WHISTLING

Here we come a-whistling through the fields so green;
Here we come a-singing, so fair to be seen.
  God send you happy, God send you happy,
  Pray God send you a happy New Year!

The roads are very dirty, my boots are very thin,
I have a little pocket to put a penny in.
  God send you happy, God send you happy,
  Pray God send you a happy New Year!

Bring out your little table and spread it with a cloth,
Bring out some of your old ale, likewise your Christmas
    loaf,
  God send you happy, God send you happy,
  Pray God send you a happy New Year!

God bless the master of this house, likewise the mistress
    too;
And all the little children that round the table strew.
  God send you happy, God send you happy,
  Pray God send you a happy New Year!

          The cock sat up in the yew tree,
            The hen came chuckling by,
          I wish you a merry Christmas,
            And a good fat pig in the sty.
                              Old Carol

MAKE WE MERRY BOTH MORE AND LESS
FOR NOW IS THE TIME OF CHRISTMAS!

Let no man come into this hall,
Groom, page, nor yet marshall,
But that some sport he bring withal!
    For now is the time of Christmas!

If that he say, he cannot sing,
Some other sport then let him bring!
That it may please at this feasting!
    For now is the time of Christmas!

If he say he can naught do,
Then for my love ask him no mo!
But to the stocks then let him go!
    For now is the time of Christmas.
        From Balliol MS. of about 1540

OUR JOYFUL FEAST

So, now is come our joyful feast,
    Let every soul be jolly!
Each room with ivy leaves is drest,
    And every post with holly.
Though some churls at our mirth repine,
Round your brows let garlands twine,
Drown sorrow in a cup of wine,
    And let us all be merry!

Now all our neighbours' chimneys smoke,
    And Christmas logs are burning;
Their ovens with baked meats do choke,
    And all their spits are turning.
Without the door let sorrow lie,
And if for cold it hap to die,
We'll bury it in Christmas pie,
    And evermore be merry!

George Wither

COME BRING WITH A NOISE

Come bring with a noise,
    My merry, merry boys,
The Christmas log to the firing;
    While my good dame, she
    Bids ye all be free,
And drink to your heart's desiring.

With the last year's brand
    Light the new block, and
For good success in his spending,
    On your psalteries play,
    That sweet luck may
Come while the log is a-tending.

Drink now the strong beer,
    Cut the white loaf here,

The while the meat is a-shredding;
  For the rare mince-pies;
  And the plums stand by,
To fill the paste that's a-kneading.
                              Robert Herrick

SIGNS OF THE SEASON IN THE KITCHEN

"The cooks shall be busied, by day and by night,
In roasting and boiling, for taste and delight,
Their senses in liquor that's happy they'll steep,
Though they be afforded to have little sleep;
They still are employed for to dress us, in brief,
Plum-pudding, goose, capon, minc'd pies, and roast
    beef.

"Although the cold weather doth hunger provoke,
'Tis a comfort to see how the chimneys do smoke;
Provision is making for beer, ale and wine,
For all that are willing or ready to dine:
Then haste to the kitchen for diet the chief,
Plum-pudding, goose, capon, minc'd pies, and roast
    beef.

"All travellers, as they do pass on their way,
At gentlemen's halls are invited to stay,
Themselves to refresh and their horses to rest,
Since that he must be old Christmas's guest;
Nay, the poor shall not want, but have for relief
Plum-pudding, goose, capon, minc'd pies, and roast
    beef."

                              Anonymous

OLD CHRISTMASTIDE

Heap on more wood!—the wind is chill;
But let it whistle as it will,
We'll keep our Christmas merry still.
Each age has deemed the new-born year
The fittest time for festal cheer.
Even, heathen yet, the savage Dane
At Iol more deep the mead did drain;
High on the beach his galleys drew,
And feasted all his pirate crew;
Then in his low and pine-built hall,
Where shields and axes decked the wall,
They gorged upon the half-dressed steer;
Caroused in seas of sable beer:
While round, in brutal jest, were thrown
The half-gnawed rib and marrow-bone,
Or listened all, in grim delight,
While Scalds yelled out the joy of fight,
Then forth in frenzy would they hie,
While wildly-loose their red locks fly:
And, dancing round the blazing pile,
They make such barbarous mirth the while,
As best might to the mind recall
The boisterous joys of Odin's hall.
And well our Christian sires of old
Loved when the year its course had rolled,
And brought blithe Christmas back again,
With all his hospitable train.
Domestic and religious rite
Gave honour to the holy night:

On Christmas Eve the bells were rung:
On Christmas Eve the mass was sung:
That only night, in all the year,
Saw the stoled priest the chalice rear.
The damsel donned her kirtle sheen:
The hall was dressed with holly green:
Forth to the woods did merry-men go,
To gather in the mistletoe:
Then opened wide the Baron's hall
To vassal, tenant, serf, and all:
Power laid his rod of rule aside,
And Ceremony doffed his pride.
The heir, with roses in his shoes,
That night might village partner choose:
The lord, underogating, share
The vulgar game of "post and pair."
All hailed, with uncontrolled delight,
And general voice, the happy night
That to the cottage, as the crown,
Brought tidings of salvation down.
The fire, with well-dried logs supplied,
Went roaring up the chimney wide:
The huge hall-table's oaken face,
Scrubbed till it shone, the day to grace,
Bore then upon its massive board
No mark to part the squire and lord.
Then was brought in the lusty brawn
By old blue-coated serving man;
Then the grim boar's head frowned on high,
Crested with bays and rosemary.
Well can the green-garbed ranger tell,

How, when, and where, the monster fell;
What dogs before his death he tore,
And all the baiting of the boar
The Wassail round, in good brown bowls,
Garnished with ribbons, blithely trowls.
There the huge sirloin reeked: hard by
Plum-porridge stood, and Christmas pie;
Nor failed old Scotland to produce,
At such high tide, her savory goose.
Then came the merry masquers in,
And carols roared with blithesome din.
If unmelodious was the song,
It was a hearty note, and strong,
Who lists may in their mumming see
Traces of ancient mystery;
White shirts supplied the masquerade,
And smutted cheeks the visors made:
But, O! what masquers, richly dight,
Can boast of bosoms half so light!
England was merry England, when
Old Christmas brought his sports again.
'Twas Christmas broached the mightiest ale;
'Twas Christmas told the merriest tale;
A Christmas gambol oft could cheer
The poor man's heart through half the year.

(*From Marmion*)

A CAROL FOR TWELFTH DAY

Mark well my heavy doleful tale,
For Twelfth Day now is come,

And now I must no longer stay,
  And say no word but mum.
For I perforce must take my leave
  Of all my dainty cheer—
Plum-porridge, roast beef and minc'd-pies,
  My strong ale and my beer.

Kind hearted Christmas, now adieu,
  For I with thee must part;
But oh! to take my leave of thee
  Doth grieve me at the heart.
Thou wert an ancient housekeeper,
  And mirth with meat didst keep,
But thou art going out of town
  Which causes me to weep.

Come, butler, fill a brimmer full,
  To cheer my fainting heart,
That to old Christmas I may drink
  Before he does depart.
And let each one that's in the room
  With me likewise condole,
And now to cheer their spirits sad
  Let each one drink a bowl.

And when the same it hath gone round,
  Then fall unto your cheer;
For you well know that Christmas time
  It comes but once a year.

Thanks to my master and my dame
That do such cheer afford,
God bless them, that each Christmas they
May furnish so their board.
                              Old English

TWELFTH NIGHT SONG

Heaped be the fagots high,
And the half-burnèd bough
From last year's revelry
Be litten now!
Brimmed be the posset bowl
For every lusty soul,
And, while the maskers rule,
Cry 'Noel,' cry 'Noel,' down all the halls of Yule!

O eager viols, thrill!
Pipe, hautboys, clear and sweet!
Work your impetuous will,
Ye restless feet!
For every lip—a glass!
For every lad—a lass!
And, ere the ardors cool,
Cry 'Noel,' cry 'Noel,' down all the halls of Yule!
                              Stephen Sennett

KING ARTHUR'S WAES-HAEL

Waes-hael for knight and dame!
O merry be their dole!

Drink-hael! in Jesu's name
  We fill the tawny bowl;
But cover down the curving crest,
Mould of the Orient Lady's breast.

Waes-hael! yet lift no lid:
  Drain ye the reeds for wine.
Drink-hael! the milk was hid
  That soothed that Babe divine;
Hushed, as this hollow channel flows,
He drew the balsam from the rose.

Waes-hael! thus glowed the breast
  Where a God yearned to cling;
Drink-hael! so Jesu pressed
  Life from its mystic spring;
Then hush, and bend in reverent sign,
And breathe the thrilling reeds for wine.

Waes-hael! in shadowy scene,
  Lo, Christmas children we!
Drink-hael! behold we lean
  At a far Mother's knee;
To dream, that thus her bosom smiled,
And learned the lip of Bethlehem's Child.
                    R. S. Hawker

THE BELLS OF CHRISTMAS

"Pilgrim, you of the loosened lachet,
  What do you hear as you roam and roam?"

"Master, I list to the bells of Christmas,
    The bells of Christmas, calling me home!

"They call and call, and I fain would hasten
    Back to the warmth of the old rooftree,
To the plentiful board and the merry faces,
    And the twilight prayer at the mother's knee!"

"Pilgrim, you of the loosened lachet,
    Why, then, still do you roam and roam?"
"Master, 'twas but a dream they conjured,
    The bells of Christmas, calling me home.

" 'Twas but a vision out of the distance,
    Happy and holy and sweet, forsooth!
'Twas but a vision out of the distance,
    Out of the long lost vale of Youth!"

"Pilgrim, you of the loosened lachet,
    All of us have our dreams like thee,
And back are borne by the bells of Christmas
    To the twilight prayer at the mother's knee!"
                    Clinton Scollard

BALLADE OF CHRISTMAS GHOSTS

Between the moonlight and the fire
    In winter twilights long ago,
What ghosts we raised for your desire,
    To make your merry blood run slow!

How old, how grave, how wise we grow!
No Christmas ghost can make us chill,
　　Save those that troop in mournful row,
The ghosts we all can raise at will!

The beasts can talk in barn and byre
　　On Christmas eve, old legends know.
As year by year the years retire,
　　We men fall silent then, I trow,
　　Such sights hath memory to show,
Such voices from the silence thrill,
　　Such shapes return with Christmas snow,—
The ghosts we all can raise at will.

Oh, children of the village choir,
　　Your carols on the midnight throw!
Oh, bright across the mist and mire,
　　Ye ruddy hearths of Christmas glow!
　　Beat back the dread, beat down the woe,
Let's cheerily descend the hill;
　　Be welcome all, to come or go,
The ghosts we all can raise at will!

ENVOY

Friends, sursum corda, soon or slow
　　We part, like guests who've joyed their fill;
Forget them not, nor mourn them so,
　　The ghosts we all can raise at will.

Andrew Lang

IX

THE CHRIST CHILD AND KRISS KRINGLE

May there not be a single
Forgotten one, Kriss Kringle,
But gifts for every child.

A CHRISTMAS CAROL FOR CHILDREN

Good news from heaven the angels bring,
Glad tidings to the earth they sing:
To us this day a Child is given,
To crown us with the joy of heaven.

This is the Christ, our God and Lord,
Who in all need shall aid afford:
He will Himself our Saviour be,
From sin and sorrow set us free.

To us that blessedness He brings,
Which from the Father's bounty springs:
That in the heavenly realm we may
With Him enjoy eternal day.

All hail, Thou noble Guest, this morn,
Whose love did not the sinner scorn!
In my distress Thou cam'st to me:
What thanks shall I return to Thee?

Were earth a thousand times as fair,
Beset with gold and jewels rare,
She yet were far too poor to be
A narrow cradle, Lord, for Thee.

Ah, dearest Jesus, Holy Child!
Make Thee a bed, soft, undefiled,
Within my heart, that it may be
A quiet chamber kept for Thee.

Praise God upon His heavenly throne,
Who gave to us His only Son:
For this His hosts, on joyful wing,
A blest New Year of mercy sing.

Martin Luther

THE FIRST CHRISTMAS

Once a little baby lay
Cradled on the fragrant hay,
Long ago on Christmas.
Stranger bed a babe ne'er found
Wondering cattle stood around,
Long ago on Christmas,
Long ago on Christmas.

By the shining vision taught,
Shepherds for the Christ-Child sought,
Long ago on Christmas.
Guided in a star-lit way
Wise men came their gifts to pay,
Long ago on Christmas,
Long ago on Christmas.

And today the whole glad earth,
Praises God for that Child's birth,

Long ago on Christmas.
For the Light, the Truth, the Way,
Came to bless the earth that day,
Long ago on Christmas,
Long ago on Christmas.

Emilie Poulsson

A CHILD'S PRAYER
(*Ex Ore Infantum*)

Little Jesus, wast Thou shy
Once, and just as small as I?
And what did it feel like to be
Out of Heaven, and just like me?
Did'st Thou sometimes think of *There*,
And ask where all the angels were?
I should think that I would cry
For my house all made of sky;
I would look about the air,
And wonder where my angels were;
And at waking 'twould distress me—
Not an angel there to dress me!

Hadst Thou ever any toys,
Like us little girls and boys?
And didst Thou play in Heaven with all
The angels, that were not too tall,
With stars for marbles? Did the things
Play *Can You See Me?* through their wings?

Didst Thou kneel at night to pray,
And didst Thou join Thy hands, this way?
And did they tire sometimes, being young,
And make the prayer seem very long?
And dost Thou like it best, that we
Should join our hands and pray to Thee?
I used to think, before I knew,
The prayer not said unless we do.

And did Thy Mother at the night
Kiss Thee and fold the clothes in right?
And didst Thou feel quite good in bed,
Kissed, and sweet, and Thy prayers said?
Thou canst not have forgotten all
That it feels like to be small;
And Thou knows't I cannot pray
To Thee in my father's way—
When Thou wast so little, say,
Coulds't Thou talk in Thy Father's way?—
So, a little child, come down
And hear a child's tongue like Thy own;
Take me by the hand and walk,
And listen to my baby talk,
To Thy Father show my prayer
(He will look, Thou art so fair),
And say: "O Father, I, Thy son,
Bring the prayer of a little one."

And He will smile, that children's tongue
Hast not changed since Thou wast young!

Francis Thompson

THE SHEPHERDS HAD AN ANGEL

The shepherds had an angel,
    The wise men had a star;
But what have I, a little child,
    To guide me home from far,
Where glad stars sing together,
    And singing angels are?

Lord Jesus is my Guardian
    So I can nothing lack;
The lambs lie in His bosom
    Along life's dangerous track:
The wilful lambs that go astray
    He, bleeding, brings them back.

Those shepherds thro' the lonely night
    Sat watching by their sheep,
Until they saw the heav'nly host
    Who neither tire nor sleep,
All singing Glory, glory,
    In festival they keep.

Christ watches me, His little lamb,
    Cares for me day and night,
That I may be His own in heav'n;
    So angels clad in white
Shall sing their Glory, glory,
    For my sake in the height.

Lord, bring me nearer day by day,
  Till I my voice unite,
And sing my Glory, glory,
  With angels clad in white.
All Glory, glory, giv'n to Thee,
  Thro' all the heav'nly height.

Christina Rossetti

A CHRISTMAS HYMN FOR CHILDREN

Our bells ring to all the earth,
  In excelsis gloria!
But none for Thee made chimes of mirth
On that great morning of Thy birth.

Our coats they lack not silk nor fur,
  In excelsis gloria!
Not such Thy blessèd Mother's were;
Full simple garments covered Her.

Our churches rise up goodly high,
  In excelsis gloria!
Low in a stall Thyself did lie,
With hornèd oxen standing by.

Incense we breathe and scent of wine,
  In excelsis gloria!
Around Thee rose the breath of kine,
Thy only drink Her breast Divine.

We take us to a happy tree,
  In excelsis gloria!
The seed was sown that day for Thee
That blossomed out of Calvary.

Teach us to feed Thy poor with meat,
  In excelsis gloria!
Who turnest not when we entreat,
Who givest us *Thy* Bread to eat.
                    Josephine Dodge Daskam

A LEGEND

Christ, when a child, a garden made,
  And many roses flourished there,
He watered them three times a day,
  To make a garland for his hair.

And when in time the roses bloomed
  He called the children in to share;
They tore the flowers from every stem
  And left the garden stript and bare.

"How wilt thou weave thyself a crown
  Now that thy roses all are dead?"
"Ye have forgotten that the thorns
  Are left for me," the Christ-child said.

They plaited then a crown of thorns
  And laid it rudely on his head.
A garland for his forehead made
  For roses drops of blood instead.
                    Tschaikovsky

THE LITTLE MUD-SPARROWS
(*Jewish Legend*)

I like that old, kind legend
    Not found in Holy Writ,
And wish that John or Matthew
    Had made Bible out of it.

But though it is not Gospel,
    There is no law to hold
The heart from growing better
    That hears the story told:—

How the little Jewish children
    Upon a summer day,
Went down across the meadows
    With the Christ Child to play.

And in the gold-green valley,
    Where low the reed-grass lay,
They made them mock mud-sparrows
    Out of the meadow clay.

So when these all were fashioned,
    And ranged in rows about,
"Now," said the little Jesus,
    "We'll let the birds fly out."

Then all the happy children
    Did call, and coax, and cry—
Each to his own mud-sparrow:
    "Fly, as I bid you! Fly!"

But earthen were the sparrows,
   And earth did they remain,
Though loud the Jewish children
   Cried out, and cried again.

Except the one bird only
   The little Christ Child made:
The earth that owned Him Master,
   —His earth heard and obeyed.

Softly he leaned and whispered:
   "Fly up to Heaven! Fly!"
And swift, His little sparrow,
   Went soaring to the sky.

And silent, all the children
   Stood, awestruck, looking on,
Till, deep into the heavens,
   The bird of earth had gone.

I like to think, for playmate
   We have the Lord Christ still,
And that still above our weakness
   He works His mighty will,

That all our little playthings
   Of earthen hopes and joys
Shall be, by His commandment,
   Changed into heavenly toys.

Our souls are like the sparrows
  Imprisoned in the clay,
Bless Him who came to give them wings
  Upon a Christmas Day!
                    Elizabeth Stuart Phelps

THE LAMB CHILD

When Christ the Babe was born,
Full many a little lamb
Upon the wintry hills forlorn
Was nestled near its dam:

And, waking or asleep
Upon His Mother's breast,
For love of her, each mother-sheep
And baby-lamb He blessed.
                    John Banister Tabb

THE LITTLE GRAY LAMB

Out on the endless purple hills, deep in the clasp of
    somber night,
The shepherds guarded their weary ones—guarded
    their flocks of snowy white,
  That like a snowdrift in silence lay,
  Save one little lamb with its fleece of gray.

Out on the hillside all alone, gazing afar with sleepless
    eyes,
The little lamb prayed soft and low, its weary face
    to the starry skies:
    "O moon of the heavens, so fair, so bright,
    Give me—oh, give me—a fleece of white!"

No answer came from the dome of blue, nor comfort
    lurked in the cypress-trees;
But faint came a whisper borne along on the scented
    wings of the passing breeze:
    "Little gray lamb that prays this night,
    I cannot give thee a fleece of white."

Then the little gray lamb of the sleepless eyes prayed
    to the clouds for a coat of snow,
Asked of the roses, besought the woods; but each gave
    answer sad and low:
    "Little gray lamb that prays this night,
    We cannot give thee a fleece of white."

Like a gem unlocked from a casket dark, like an ocean
    pearl from its bed of blue,
Came, softly stealing the clouds between, a wonderful
    star which brighter grew,
    Until it flamed like the sun by day
    Over the place where Jesus lay.

Ere hushed were the angels' notes of praise, the joyful
    shepherds had quickly sped

Past rock and shadow, adown the hill, to kneel at the
    Saviour's lowly bed;
  While, like the spirits of phantom night,
  Followed their flocks—their flocks of white.

And patiently, longingly, out of the night, apart from
    the others,—far apart,—
Came limping and sorrowful, all alone, the little gray
    lamb of the weary heart,
  Murmuring, "I must bide far away:
  I am not worthy—my fleece is gray."

And the Christ Child looked upon humbled pride, at
    kings bent low on the earthen floor,
But gazed beyond at the saddened heart of the little
    gray lamb at the open door;
And he called it up to his manger low and laid his
    hand on its wrinkled face,
While the kings drew golden robes aside to give to
    the weary one a place.
  And the fleece of the little gray lamb was blest:
  For, lo! it was whiter than all the rest!

In many cathedrals grand and dim, whose windows
    glimmer with pane and lens,
Mid the odor of incense raised in prayer, hallowed
    about with last amens,
The infant Saviour is pictured fair, with kneeling Magi
    wise and old,

But his baby-hand rests—not on the gifts, the myrrh,
   the frankincense, the gold—
But on the head, with a heavenly light,
Of the little gray lamb that was changed to white.
                Archibald Beresford Sullivan

THE CRECHE

Gabriel had gathered moss,
   Justine a tiny tree,
Francoise patted out the sand
   Where Jean Baptiste could see.

They built the little stable up
   And hung the golden star,
They set the tree and spread the moss
   And viewed it from afar.

Their fingers trembled on the box
   That held the holy things—
They took the Blessed Baby out
   And dusted off the Kings.

They made a little shining pool
   From a looking glass;
Francoise placed the shepherd lads,
   Justine the weary ass.

Joseph and heaven-blue Mary fell
   To eldest Gabriel—
The others crowded close to see
   That he placed them well.

Between these two the dimpled hands
  Of little Jean Baptiste
Laid the smiling Jesus down—
  The mightiest to the least.

When it was done they stood about
  All silent in their places,
And years and seas dissolved before
  The still light in their faces.

One said "Joli!" and one said "Bien!"
  A radiance shone on them
As shone once on the shepherd lads
  In far-off Bethlehem.

Carol Ryrie Brink

CAROL OF THE RUSSIAN CHILDREN

Snow-bound mountains, snow-bound valleys,
Snow-bound plateaus, clad in white,
Fur-robed moujiks, fur-robed nobles,
Fur-robed children, see the light.

Shaggy pony, shaggy oxen,
Gentle shepherds, wait the light;
Little Jesus, little Mother,
Good St. Joseph, come this night.
Light! Light! Light!

Russian Folk Song

THE WAITS

There were sparkles on the window-pane and sparkles
    in the sky,
The moon it sparkled like a star above the world so
    high,
There was star-shine on the ceiling, there was star-shine
    on the bed,
There was star-shine in my eyes, I think, and star-shine
    in my head.
I clambered from my sleep, I did; I flung the window
    wide,
I wanted all that waited in the Christmas Eve outside,
I wanted for myself to hear the Christmas people sing,
I wanted for myself to hear the Christmas joy-bells
    ring.
And there outside were waiting three grey Shepherds
    in the snow,
(I knew that they were Shepherds, for they all had
    crooks, you know,)
And when they saw me waiting too they sang to me a
    song—
The stars, they caught and whispered it the whole
    wide sky along.
And then the Shepherds went their way and three
    black camels came,
They stayed beneath the window there and waited just
    the same,
And each black camel on his back had brought an
    Eastern King,

And though each King was very great each had a song
    to sing.
They sang it as the Shepherds sang, a little low sweet
    song,—
The white stars caught and whispered it the whole
    wide sky along;
And then the camels went their way, I watched them
    down the street,
The snow lay white and soft and still beneath their
    silent feet.
There was singing in the tree-tops, there was singing
    in the sky,
The moon was singing to the clouds above the world
    so high,
And all the stars were singing too and when I looked
    below,
I saw a little, tiny Child was waiting in the snow.
And first I watched him wait there, watched and only
    waved my hand,
For though the song was in my heart I did not under-
    stand,
Until at last it burst in words, because at last I knew,
And then he looked at me and laughed and sang the
    star-song too.
And right across the misty fields I heard the church
    bells ring,
The star-song echoed far and wide for all the world
    to sing,
And still the tiny Child stood there—the Child that
    once was born—

We sang His birthday song—we did—upon His Christmas morn.

M. Nightingale

PRAYER

Last night I crept across the snow,
Where only tracking rabbits go,
And then I waited quite alone
Until the Christmas radiance shone!

At midnight twenty angels came,
Each white and shining like a flame.
At midnight twenty angels sang,
The stars swung out like bells and rang.

They lifted me across the hill,
They bore me in their arms until
A greater glory greeted them.
It was the town of Bethlehem.

And gently, then, they set me down,
All worshipping that holy town,
And gently, then, they bade me raise
My head to worship and to praise.

And gently, then the Christ smiled down.
Ah, there was glory in that town!
It was as if the world were free
And glistening with purity.

And in that vault of crystal blue,
It was as if the world were new,
And myriad angels, file on file,
Gloried in the Christ-child's smile.

It was so beautiful to see
Such glory, for a child like me,
So beautiful, it does not seem
It could have been a Christmas dream.

John Farrar

CHRISTMAS TREASURES

I count my treasures o'er with care,
   The little toy my darling knew,
   A little sock of faded hue,
A little lock of golden hair.

Long years ago this holy time,
   My little one—my all to me—
   Sat robed in white upon my knee
And heard the merry Christmas chime.

"Tell me, my little golden-head,
   If Santa Claus should come tonight,
   What shall he bring my baby bright,—
What treasure for my boy?" I said.

And then he named this little toy,
   While in his round and mournful eyes
   There came a look of sweet surprise,
That spoke his quiet, trustful joy.

And as he lisped his evening prayer
  He asked the boon with childish grace,
  Then, toddling to the chimney place,
He hung his little stocking there.

That night, while lengthening shadows crept,
  I saw the white-robed angels come
  With singing to our lowly home
And kiss my darling as he slept.

They must have heard his little prayer,
  For in the morn, with rapturous face,
  He toddled to the chimney-place,
And found this little treasure there.

They came again one Christmas-tide,—
  That angel host, so fair and white!
  And singing all that glorious night,
They lured my darling from my side.

A little sock, a little toy,
  A little lock of golden hair,
  The Christmas music on the air,
A watching for my baby boy!

But if again that angel train
  And golden-head come back for me,
  To bear me to Eternity,
My watching will not be in vain!

                    Eugene Field

A CHRISTMAS SONG

Oh, Christmas is a jolly time
   When forests hang with snow,
And other forests bend with toys,
   And lordly Yule logs glow.

And Christmas is a solemn time
   Because, beneath the star,
The first great Christmas Gift was given
   To all men, near and far.

But not alone at Christmas time
   Comes holiday and cheer,
For one who loves a little child
   Hath Christmas all the year.

Florence Evelyn Dratt

CHRISTMAS CAROL

The earth has grown old with its burden of care,
   But at Christmas it always is young,
The heart of the jewel burns lustrous and fair,
And its soul full of music bursts forth on the air,
   When the song of the angels is sung.

It is coming, Old Earth, it is coming to-night!
   On the snowflakes which cover thy sod.
The feet of the Christ-child fall gentle and white,.
And the voice of the Christ-child tells out with delight
   That mankind are the children of God.

On the sad and the lonely, the wretched and poor,
  The voice of the Christ-child shall fall;
And to every blind wanderer open the door
Of hope that he dared not to dream of before,
  With a sunshine of welcome for all.

The feet of the humblest may walk in the field
  Where the feet of the Holiest trod,
This, then, is the marvel to mortals revealed
When the silvery trumpets of Christmas have pealed,
  That mankind are the children of God.

Phillips Brooks

SIGNS OF CHRISTMAS

When on the barn's thatch'd roof is seen
The moss in tufts of liveliest green;
When Roger to the wood pile goes,
And, as he turns, his fingers blows;
When all around is cold and drear,
Be sure that Christmas-tide is near.

When up the garden walk in vain
We seek for Flora's lovely train;
When the sweet hawthorn bower is bare,
And bleak and cheerless is the air;
When all seems desolate around,
Christmas advances o'er the ground.

When Tom at eve come home from plough,
And brings the mistletoe's green bough,
With milk-white berries spotted o'er,
And shakes it the sly maids before,
Then hangs the trophy up on high,
Be sure that Christmas-tide is nigh.

When Hal, the woodman, in his clogs,
Bears home the huge unwieldy logs,
That, hissing on the smouldering fire,
Flame out at last a quiv'ring spire;
When in his hat the holly stands,
Old Christmas musters up his bands.

When cluster'd round the fire at night,
Old William talks of ghost and sprite,
And as a distant out-house gate
Slams by the wind, they fearful wait,
While some each shadowy nook explore,
Then Christmas pauses at the door.

When Dick comes shiv'ring from the yard,
And says the pond is frozen hard,
While from his hat, all white with snow,
The moisture, trickling, drops below,
While carols sound, the night to cheer,
Then Christmas and his train are here.

                              Edwin Lees

JOIN THE CAROLING

Come out and join the caroling,
Good friends and neighbors jolly!
Across the candle-lighted snow,
A troop of singers we shall go
And stop 'neath magic mistletoe
  Or laughing wreaths of holly,
To sing the songs of yesteryear,
That old and young delight to hear.

The snow will hush our eager feet,
And we shall fill the silent street
  With bursts of happy song,
That those who sleep may dream more sweet,
  Because we pass along;
That those who wake true joy may take
In this our festive throng.

The hollow night will be our bowl,
  The wind, our wassail stinging;
Good will flows forth from soul to soul
As underneath the stars we stroll
  Exultant in our singing.

But when the chimes in yonder tower
Give warning of the midnight hour,
The winding way we shall retrace
And, with a good-night's parting grace,
Shall leave the frosty skies behind,
  And each a hearty welcome find
Within the Yule-log's warm embrace.

Come out and join the caroling,
  Good friends and neighbors jolly—
Come! let us wreath the world in song
  More brilliant than the holly!

                    Rowena Bastin Bennett

CHRISTMAS EVE

All night long the pine-trees wait,
  Dark heads bowed in solemn state,
Wondering what may be the fate
  Of little Norway Spruce.

Little Norway Spruce who stood
Only lately in the wood.
Did they take him for his good—
  They who bore him off?

Little Norway Spruce so trim,
Lithe, and free, and strong of limb—
All the pines were proud of him!
  Now his place is bare!

All that night the little tree
In the dark stood patiently,
Far away from forest free,
  Laden for the morn.

Chained and laden, but intent,
On the pines his thoughts were bent;
They might tell him what it meant,
  If he could but go!

Morning came—the children. "See!
Oh, our glorious Christmas-tree!"
Gifts for everyone had he;
    Then he understood.

Mary Mapes Dodge

SONG OF THE CHRISTMAS TREES

Oho for the woods where I used to grow,
The home of the lonely owl and crow!
I spread my arms to shelter all
The creatures shy, both large and small.
I sang for joy to the friends I knew;
The sunshine, rain and the sky so blue.
Oho for the forest! Oho for the hills!
Oho for the ripples of murmuring rills!
    Oho, sing I, oho!

Oho for the hall where I now hold sway,
The home of the happy children gay!
I spread my arms with gifts for all,
From father big to baby small.
I sing for joy to these hearts that glow—
Of manger bed, and the Child we know.
Oho for the holly! Oho for the light!
Oho for the mistletoe's berries so white!
    Oho, sing I, oho!

Blanche Elizabeth Wade

SONG

"I know, I know
Where the green leaves grow,
When the woods without are bare;
Where a sweet perfume
Of the woodland's bloom
Is afloat on the winter's air:
When tempest strong
Has howled along
With his war whoop wild and loud,
Till the broad ribs broke
Of the forest oak,
And his crown of glory bowed.

"I know, I know
Where the green leaves grow,
Though the groves without are bare;
Where the branches nod
Of the trees of God,
And the wild vines flourish fair.
For a fragrant crown
When the Lord comes down
Of the deathless green we braid,
O'er the altar bright,
Where the tissue white
Like the winter's snow is laid.

"And we think it meet
Our Lord to greet,
As the wise men did of old,
With the spiceries of incense trees,

And hearts like hoarded gold.
  And so we shake
  The snowy flake
From cedar and myrtle fair,
  And the boughs that nod
  On the hills of God
We raise to His glory there."

Arthur Cleveland Coxe

THE LITTLE CHRISTMAS TREE

The Christmas Day was coming, the Christmas Eve
  drew near,
The fir-trees, they were talking low at midnight, cold
  and clear;
And this is what the fir-trees said, all in the pale
  moonlight;
"Now, which of us shall chosen be to grace the holy
  night?"

The tall trees and the goodly trees raised each a lofty
  head,
In glad and secret confidence, though not a word they
  said.
But one, the baby of the band, could not restrain a
  sigh—
"You all will be approved," he said, "but oh! what
  chance have I?'

"I am so small, so very small, no one will mark or
  know

How thick and green my needles are, how true my
    branches grow.
Few toys and candles could I hold, but heart and will
    are free,
And in my heart of hearts I know I am a Christmas
    tree."

The Christmas angel hovered near; he caught the
    grieving word,
And, laughing low, he hurried forth, with love and
    pity stirred.
He sought and found St. Nicholas, the dear old
    Christmas saint,
And in his fatherly, kind ear, rehearsed the fir-tree's
    plaint.

Saints are all-powerful, we know, so it befell that day
That, axe on shoulder, to the grove a woodman took
    his way.
One baby girl he had at home, and he went forth to
    find
A little tree as small as she, just suited to his mind.

Oh! glad and proud the baby-fir, amid its brethren
    tall,
To be thus chosen and singled out, the first among
    them all!
He stretched his fragrant branches, his little heart
    beat fast;
He was a truly Christmas tree—he had his wish at
    last.

One large and shining apple, with cheeks of ruddy
    gold;
Six tapers, and a tiny doll were all that he could hold.
The baby laughed, the baby crowed, to see the tapers
    bright;
The forest baby felt the joy, and shared in the delight.

And when at last, the tapers died, and when the baby
    slept,
The little fir, in silent night, a patient vigil kept.
Though scorched and brown its needles were, it had
    no heart to grieve,
"I have not lived in vain," he said; "thank God for
    Christmas Eve!"

Susan Coolidge

A CHRISTMAS CAROL

Everywhere, everywhere, Christmas tonight!
Christmas in lands of the fir-tree and pine,
Christmas in lands of the palm-tree and vine,
Christmas where snow-peaks stand solemn and white,
Christmas where cornfields lie sunny and bright,
    Everywhere, everywhere, Christmas tonight!

Christmas where children are hopeful and gay,
Christmas where old men are patient and gray,
Christmas where peace, like a dove in its flight,
Broods o'er brave men in the thick of the fight.
    Everywhere, everywhere, Christmas tonight!

For the Christ-child who comes is the Master of all,
No palace too great and no cottage too small;
The angels who welcome Him sing from the height,
"In the city of David, a King in His might."
    Everywhere, everywhere, Christmas tonight!

Then let every heart keep its Christmas within,
Christ's pity for sorrow, Christ's hatred for sin,
Christ's care for the weakest, Christ's courage for right
Christ's dread of the darkness, Christ's love of the light,
    Everywhere, everywhere, Christmas tonight!

So the stars of the midnight which compass us round
Shall see a strange glory, and hear a sweet sound,
And cry, "Look! the earth is aflame with delight,
O sons of the morning, rejoice at the sight."
    Everywhere, everywhere, Christmas tonight!

Phillips Brooks

THE MAGIC MONTH

This is the magic month of all the year,
    Holding the children's golden, precious day,
    Of which, with eager eyes we hear them say:
"In three weeks—two weeks—one week—'twill be
    here!"
The sparkling windows of the shops appear
    In fascinating, wonder-bright array;
    With holly and with greens, the streets are gay;
The bustling town begins its Christmas cheer.

Now secret plots are whispered in the hall;
Mysterious parcels to the door are brought,
  And busy hands are half-done gifts concealing;
The Eve is here, with merriment for all,
And Santa Claus, with merry marvels fraught,
  Before the dawn across the roofs comes stealing.

Gelett Burgess

JEST 'FORE CHRISTMAS

Father calls me William, sister calls me Will,
Mother calls me Willie, but the fellers call me Bill!
Mighty glad I ain't a girl—ruther be a boy,
Without them sashes, curls, an' things that's worn by
    Fauntleroy!
Love to chawnk green apples an' go swimmin' in the
    lake—
Hate to take the caster-ile they give for belly-ache!
'Most all the time, the whole year round, there ain't
    no flies on me,
But jest 'fore Christmas I'm as good as I kin be!

Got a yeller dog named Sport, sic him on the cat;
First thing she knows she doesn't know where she is at;
Got a clipper sled, an' when us kids goes out to slide,
'Long comes the grocery cart, an' we all hook a ride!
And sometimes when the grocery man is worrited an'
    cross,
He reaches at us with his whip, an' larrups up his hoss,
An' then I laff an' holler, "Oh, ye never teched me!"
But jest 'fore Christmas I'm as good as I kin be!

Gran'ma says she hopes that when I git to be a man,
I'll be a missionarer like her oldest brother, Dan,
As was et up by the cannibuls that live in Ceylon's
        Isle,
Where every prospeck pleases, an' only man is vile!
But gran'ma she has never been to see a Wild West
        Show,
Nor read the life of Daniel Boone, or else I guess she'd
        know
That Buff'lo Bill and cowboys is good enough for me!
Excep' jest 'fore Christmas, when I'm good as I kin be!

And then old Sport he hangs around, so solemn-like an'
        still,
His eyes they keep a-sayin': "What's the matter, little
        Bill?"
The old cat sneaks down off her perch an' wonders
        what's become
Of them two enemies of hern that used to make things
        hum!
But I am so perlite an' 'tend so earnestly to biz,
That mother says to father: "How improved our Willie
        is!"
But father, havin' been a boy hisself, kind of suspicions
        me
When, jest 'fore Christmas, I'm as good as I kin be!

For Christmas, with its lots an' lots of candies, cakes,
        an' toys,
Was made, they say, for proper kids an' not for naughty
        boys;

So wash yer face an' bresh yer hair, an' mind yer p's
    and q's,
An' don't bust out yer pantaloons, an' don't wear out
    yer shoes;
Say "Yessum" to the ladies, an' "Yessur" to the men,
An' when they's company, don't pass yer plate for pie
    again;
But, thinkin' of the thing yer'd like to see upon that
    tree,
Jest 'fore Christmas be as good as yer kin be!

Eugene Field

A VISIT FROM ST. NICHOLAS

'Twas the night before Christmas, when all through
    the house
Not a creature was stirring, not even a mouse;
The stockings were hung by the chimney with care,
In hopes that St. Nicholas soon would be there;
The children were nestled all snug in their beds,
While visions of sugar-plums danced through their
    heads;
And mamma in her kerchief, and I in my cap,
Had just settled our brains for a long winter's nap,—
When out on the lawn there arose such a clatter,
I sprang from my bed to see what was the matter.
Away to the window I flew like a flash,
Tore open the shutters and threw up the sash.
The moon, on the breast of the new-fallen snow,
Gave a lustre of midday to objects below;

When what to my wondering eyes should appear,
But a miniature sleigh and eight tiny reindeer,
With a little old driver so lively and quick
I knew in a moment it must be St. Nick.
More rapid than eagles his coursers they came,
And he whistled and shouted and called them by
     name:
"Now, Dasher! now, Dancer! now, Prancer and Vixen!
On, Comet! on, Cupid! on, Donder and Blitzen!
To the top of the porch, to the top of the wall!
Now, dash away, dash away, dash away all!"
As dry leaves that before the wild hurricane fly,
When they meet with an obstacle, mount to the sky,
So, up to the house-top the coursers they flew,
With a sleigh full of toys,—and St. Nicholas too.
And then in a twinkling I heard on the roof
The prancing and pawing of each little hoof.
As I drew in my head and was turning around,
Down the chimney St. Nicholas came with a bound.
He was dressed all in fur from his head to his foot,
And his clothes were all tarnished with ashes and soot;
A bundle of toys he had flung on his back,
And he looked like a peddler just opening his pack.
His eyes how they twinkled! his dimples how merry!
His cheeks were like roses, his nose like a cherry;
His droll little mouth was drawn up like a bow,
And the beard on his chin was as white as the snow.
The stump of a pipe he held tight in his teeth,
And the smoke it encircled his head like a wreath.
He had a broad face, and a little round belly
That shook, when he laughed, like a bowl full of jelly.

He was chubby and plump,—a right jolly old elf—
And I laughed when I saw him, in spite of myself.
A wink of his eye and a twist of his head
Soon gave me to know I had nothing to dread.
He spoke not a word, but went straight to his work,
And filled all the stockings; then turned with a jerk,
And laying his finger aside of his nose,
And giving a nod, up the chimney he rose.
He sprang to his sleigh, to his team gave a whistle,
And away they all flew like the down of a thistle;
But I heard him exclaim, ere he drove out of sight:
"Happy Christmas to all, and to all a good-night!"

Clement C. Moore

SANTA CLAUS' PETITION

Dear Children,—I write in great haste just to say
I've met with an accident coming this way.
As Christmas is near, and I've so much to do,
I really must beg a slight favor of you;
And, unless I mistake, the small folks of this nation
Will spare poor old Santa great mortification
By setting about with their might and their main
To see that the accident's righted again.
You know, I suppose, that the distance is great
I travel each year; and for fear I'll be late,
I whip up my reindeer, and make each good steed
Go prancing along at the top of his speed.
This year my big sleigh was as full as 't could hold;
I wrapped me up warm—for the weather was cold—

And started once more on my gay Christmas tour
With lightest of hearts, you may be quite sure.
Hi! how the bells jingled and mingled in tune!
I bowed to the stars and winked at the moon.
I found myself crossing the great open sea,
With dolphins and merchildren gazing at me;
I bent a bit over the side of my sleigh
To wave them a hand, when—ah me lackaday!—
A stocking crammed full to the very small toe
Fell over the back to the sea down below,
And there the merchildren made merry ado
With toys I had meant for some dear one of you.
So this is my accident, and I would ask—
I know you won't deem it a troublesome task—
That if you should see some poor child with no toys
Upon Christmas morning, dear girls and dear boys,
You'll know the fat stocking he was to have had
Is deep in the sea and poor Santa is sad,
And see that the accident's righted, because
'Twill be a great favor to

Yours,

Santa Claus.

Julie M. Lippmann

SHOE OR STOCKING

In Holland, children set their shoes,
   This night, outside the door;
These wooden shoes, Knecht Clobes sees,
   And fills them from his store.

But here we hang our stockings up
    On handy hook or nail;
And Santa Claus, when all is still,
    Will plump them, without fail.

Speak out, you "Sober-sides," speak out,
    And let us hear your views;
Between a stocking and a shoe,
    What do you see to choose?

One instant pauses Sober-sides,
    A little sigh to fetch—
"Well, seems to me a stocking's best,
    For wooden shoes won't stretch."

                    Edith M. Thomas

KRISS KRINGLE

Just as the moon was fading
    Amid her misty rings,
And every stocking was stuffed
    With childhood's precious things.

Old Kriss Kringle looked round,
    And saw on the elm-tree bough,
High-hung an oriole's nest,
    Silent and empty now.

"Quite like a stocking," he laughed,
    "Pinned up there on the tree!

Little I thought the birds
Expected a present from me!"

Then old Kriss Kringle, who loves
A joke as well as the best,
Dropped a handful of flakes
In the oriole's empty nest.

Thomas Bailey Aldrich

CHRISTMAS EVE

The children dreamed the whole night through
Of stockings hung the hearth beside;
And bound to make each dream come true
Went Santa Claus at Christmas-tide.

Black stockings, red, brown, white and gray—
Long, little, warm, or patched and thin—
The kindly saint found on his way,
And, smiling, popped his presents in.

But as he felt his hoard grow light,
A tear-drop glistened in his eye,
"More children on this earth tonight
Than stars are twinkling in the sky."

Upon the white and frozen snow
He knelt, his empty bag beside—
"Some little socks must empty go,
Alas!" said he, "this Christmas-tide.

"Though I their stockings may not heap
    With gifts and joys and Christmas cheer,
These little ones from sorrow keep;
    For each, dear Lord, to Thee is dear!

"Thou wert a little child like them,"
    Prayed he, "for whom I would provide,
Long years ago in Bethlehem,
    That first and blessed Christmas-tide.

"As soothed Thee, then, Thy mother's kiss,
    And all her comfort sweet and kind,
So give them love, lest they may miss
    The gifts I know not where to find.

"That sweetest gift, dear Lord, bestow
    On all the children far and wide;
And give them hearts as pure as snow,"
    Prayed Santa Claus—at Christmas-tide.
                                    Marguerite Merington

WAYSIDE MUSIC

As little children in a darkened hall
    At Christmas-tide await the opening door,
Eager to tread the fairy-haunted floor
About the tree with goodly gifts for all,
And in the dark unto each other call—
Trying to guess their happiness before,—
Or of their elders eagerly implore,—
Hints of what fortune unto them may fall:

So wait we in Time's dim and narrow room,
And with strange fancies, or another's thought,
Try to divine, before the curtain rise,
The wondrous scene. Yet soon shall fly the gloom,
And we shall see what patient ages sought,
The Father's long-planned gift of Paradise.

Charles Henry Crandall

X

THE MESSAGE OF CHRISTMAS TO OUR
OWN TIME

Now is the holy not afar
In temples lighted by a star,
But where the loves and labors are.

GOOD KING WENCESLAS

Good King Wenceslas look'd out
On the Feast of Stephen,
When the snow lay round about,
Deep, and crisp, and even:
Brightly shone the moon that night,
Though the frost was cruel,
When a poor man came in sight,
Gath'ring winter fuel.

"Hither, page, and stand by me,
    If thou know'st it, telling,
Yonder peasant, who is he?
    Where and what his dwelling?"
"Sire, he lives a good league hence,
    Underneath the mountain;
Right against the forest fence,
    By Saint Agnes' fountain."

"Bring me flesh, and bring me wine,
    Bring me pine-logs hither;
Thou and I shall see him dine,
    When we bear them thither."
Page and monarch forth they went,
    Forth they went together;
Through the rude wind's wild lament:
    And the bitter weather.

"Sire, the night is darker now,
　And the wind blows stronger;
Fails my heart, I know not how,
　I can go no longer."
"Mark my footsteps, good my page,
　Tread thou in them boldly:
Thou shalt find the winter's rage
　Freeze thy blood less coldly."

In his master's steps he trod,
Where the snow lay dinted;
Heat was in the very sod
Where the saint had printed.
Therefore, Christian men, be sure,
Wealth or rank possessing,
Ye who now will bless the poor,
Shall yourselves find blessing.
　　　Translated from the Latin by J. M. Neale

COURTESY

Of Courtesy, it is much less
Than Courage of Heart or Holiness,
Yet in my Walks it seems to me
That the Grace of God is in Courtesy.

On Monks I did in Storrington fall,
They took me straight into their Hall;
I saw Three Pictures on a wall,
And Courtesy was in them all.

The first Annunciation;
The second the Visitation;
The third the Consolation,
Of God that was Our Lady's Son.

The first was of Saint Gabriel;
On Wings a-flame from Heaven he fell;
And as he went upon one knee
He shone with Heavenly Courtesy.

Our Lady out of Nazareth rode—
It was her month of heavy load;
Yet was Her Face both great and kind,
For Courtesy was in Her Mind.

The third it was our Little Lord,
Whom all the Kings in arms adored;
He was so small you could not see
His large intent of Courtesy.

Our Lord, that was Our Lady's Son,
Go bless you, People, one by one;
My Rhyme is written, my work is done.
Hilaire Belloc

THAT HOLY THING

They all were looking for a king
  To slay their foes and lift them high;
Thou cam'st, a little baby thing
  That made a woman cry.

O Son of Man, to right my lot
    Naught but Thy presence can avail:
Yet on the road Thy wheels are not,
    Nor on the sea Thy sail!

My how or when Thou wilt not heed,
    But come down Thine own secret stair,
That Thou mayst answer all my need—
    Yea, every bygone prayer.
                                George MacDonald

GRACIOUS SAVIOUR BORN OF MARY

Gracious Saviour, born of Mary;
Born to know the hours of weakness
Of the babe that thirsts and hungers,
Of the child whose feet are weary,
And whose heart grows sad and troubled
As the shadows slowly gather;
We as children kneel before Thee;
In Thy graciousness enfold us;
Keep our feet from wandering blindly;
    Give us light.

Mighty Saviour, born to victory;
Born to know fierce throes of conflict,
Lonely vigils on the mountain,
Nights of prayer when men were sleeping,
And to save men from the thralldom

Of their own mad lusts for evil;
Torn with strife we come before Thee;
In Thy mightiness enfold us;
Keep our timid hearts from fainting
  Give us strength.

Holy Saviour, born to sorrow,
Born to see the haunting shadow
Of the Cross that loomed before Thee,
Long, long years before Thy Passion;
Born to suffer wrath and hatred
And to answer scorn with pity;
Burdened with our sins we seek Thee;
In Thy holiness enfold us;
Lay Thy healing cross upon us;
  Give us peace.

Edmund Hamilton Sears, 2nd

A BALLAD OF CHRISTMAS

It was about the deep of night,
  And still was earth and sky,
When 'neath the moonlight dazzling bright,
  Three ghosts came riding by.

Beyond the sea, beyond the sea,
  Lie kingdoms for them all:
I wot their steeds trod wearily—
  The journey was not small.

By rock and desert, sand and stream,
　　They footsore late did go:
Now like a sweet and blessed dream
　　Their path was deep with snow.

Shining like hoar-frost rode they on,
　　Three ghosts in earth's array;
It was about the hour when wan
　　Night turns at hint of day.

Oh, but their hearts with woe distraught
　　Hailed not the wane of night,
Only for Jesu still they sought
　　To wash them clean and white.

For bloody was each hand, and dark
　　With death each orbless eye;—
It was three traitors mute and stark
　　Came riding silent by.

Silver their raiment and their spurs,
　　And silver-shod their feet,
And silver-pale each face that stares
　　Into the moonlight sweet.

And he upon the left that rose
　　Was Pilate, Prince of Rome,
Whose journey once lay far abroad
　　And now was nearing home.

And he upon the right that rode
  Herod of Salem sate,
Whose mantle dipped in children's blood
  Shone clear as Heaven's gate.

And he these twain betwixt that rode
  Was clad as white as wool,
Dyed in the Mercy of his God
  White was he crown to sole.

Throned mid a myriad saints in bliss
  Rise shall the Babe of Heaven
To shine on these three ghosts, I wis,
  Smit thro' with sorrows seven.

Babe of the Blessèd Trinity
  Shall smile their steeds to see:
Herod and Pilate riding by,
  And Judas one of three.

                              Walter de la Mare

SHALL I TO THE BYRE GO DOWN

Shall I to the byre go down
  Where the stalled oxen are?
Or shall I climb the mountain's crown
  To see the rising star?
Or shall I walk the golden floor
  Where the King's feast is spread?

Or shall I seek the poor man's door
    And ask to break his bread?

It matters not. Go where you will,
    Kneel down in cattle stall,
Climb up the cold and starlit hill,
    Enter in hut or hall,
To the warm fireside give your cheek,
    Or turn it to the snow,
It matters not; the One you seek
    You'll find where'er you go.

His sandal-sole is on the earth,
    His head is in the sky,
His voice is in the baby's mirth
    And in the old man's sigh,
His shadow falls across the sea,
    His breath is in the wind,
His tears with all who grieve left He,
    His heart with all who sinned.

Whether you share the poor man's mite
    Or taste the king's own fare,
He whom you go to seek tonight
    Will meet you everywhere;
For He is where the cattle wend,
    And where the planets shine—
Lo, He is in your eyes! Oh friend,
    Stand still, and look in mine.

Eleanor Farjeon

A TOAST

The many do not break their bread with us
    Their chalice is not ours, they do not seek
Our faces. Daily, in the crowded ways,
    They pass and do not speak.

They are too rich, perhaps, and we too poor,
    Perhaps they are too young and we too old,
Perhaps they are too plain and we too proud,
    Too scornful or too cold.

And yet,—for all, one toast at Christmas time,
    When Merriment her utmost bounty spends;
God bless the many who are not the few!
    God bless the few—our friends!

Marguerite Wilkinson

A CHRISTMAS WISH

Thine own wish wish I thee in every place—
    The Christmas joy, the song, the feast, the cheer:
Thine be the light of love in every face
That looks on thee to bless thy coming year.
Thine own wish wish I thee—what dost thou crave?
    All thy dear hopes be thine, whate'er they be.
A wish fulfilled may make thee king or slave;
    I wish thee wisdom's eyes wherewith to see.

Behold, she stands and waits, the youthful Year!
   A breeze of morning breathes about her brows:
She holds the storm and sunshine, bliss and fear.
   Blossoms and fruit upon the ending boughs,
She brings thee gifts. What blessing wilt thou choose?
   Life's crown of good in earth or Heaven above?
The one immortal joy thou canst not lose
   Is love! Leave all the rest, and choose thou love.

Celia Thaxter

A BELL

   Had I the power
   To cast a bell that should from some great tower,
   At the first Christmas hour,
   Out-ring,
   And fling
   A jubilant message wide,
   The forgèd metals should be thus allied;—
   No iron Pride,
   But soft Humility and rich-veined Hope
   Cleft from a sunny slope,
   And there should be
   White Charity,
   And silvery Love that knows not Doubt nor Fear,
   To make the peal more clear;
   And then, to firmly fix the fine alloy,
   There should be Joy!

Clinton Scollard

THE DEATHLESS TALE

Had He not breathed His breath
Truly at Nazareth;
Had not His very feet
Roamed many a hill and street;
Had Mary's Story gone
To Time's oblivion;
Had the sweet record paled
And the truth not prevailed:
Dormant and bleak had been
This transitory scene,
And dark, thrice dark our earth
Unknowing of His birth.

The flowers beheld His face,
The stars knew His white grace.
The grass was greener for
His humble stable door;
The rose upon its stem
Redder for Bethlehem.
And we—are we not wise
To cling with avid eyes
To the old tale, and be
Moved by its memory?
Unutterably dim
Our bright world, lacking Him.

Charles Hanson Towne

"—TO ALL PEOPLE"

So long ago, and not forgotten yet!
   Shall we remember other things as well
   As that faint whispered foreign syllable
Of rapture which the winds of heaven met
And bore like light from a sun quick to set
   To every lonely peak and crowded fell,
   The golden whisper of a miracle
Men dare to know and do not dare forget?

Shall all the sounding tempests of red war,
   The clangor of stern empire, the soft notes
      Of lovers, or the poet's lonely horn,
Ring with a noise perpetual and far
   As that soft whisper out of heaven's throats
      That said, "Lo, unto you the Christ is born"?

Clement Wood

CHRISTMAS BELLS

I heard the bells on Christmas Day
Their old, familiar carols play,
   And wild and sweet
   The words repeat
Of peace on earth, good-will to men!

And thought how, as the day had come,
The belfries of all Christendom

Had rolled along
The unbroken song
Of peace on earth, good-will to men!

Till, ringing, singing on its way,
The world revolved from night to day,
   A voice, a chime,
   A chant sublime
Of peace on earth, good-will to men!

Then from each black, accursed mouth
The cannon thundered in the South,
   And with the sound
   The carols drowned
Of peace on earth, good-will to men!

It was as if an earthquake rent
The hearth-stones of a continent,
   And made forlorn
   The households born
Of peace on earth, good-will to men!

And in despair I bowed my head:
"There is no peace on earth," I said,
   "For hate is strong,
   And mocks the song
Of peace on earth, good-will to men!"

Then pealed the bells more loud and deep:
"God is not dead; nor doth he sleep!

The wrong shall fail
The right prevail,
With peace on earth, good-will to men!"
Henry Wadsworth Longfellow

A CHRISTMAS CARMEN

Sound over all waters, reach out from all lands,
The chorus of voices, the clasping of hands;
Sing hymns that were sung by the stars of the morn,
Sing songs of the angels when Jesus was born!
　With glad jubilations
　Bring hope to the nations!
The dark night is ending and dawn has begun:
Rise, hope of the ages, arise like the sun,
　All speech flow to music, all hearts beat as one!

Sing the bridal of nations! with chorals of love;
Sing out the war-vulture and sing in the dove,
Till the hearts of the people keep time in accord,
And the voice of the world is the voice of the Lord!
　Clasp hands of the nations
　In strong gratulations:
The dark night is ending and dawn has begun;
Rise, hope of the ages, arise like the sun.
　All speech flow to music, all hearts beat as one!

Blow bugles of battle, the marches of peace;
East, west, north and south, let the long quarrel cease:
Sing the song of great joy that the angels began,
Sing of glory to God and of good-will to man!

Hark, joining in chorus
The heavens bend o'er us!
The dark night is ending and dawn has begun:
Rise, hope of all ages, arise like the sun,
All speech flow to music, all hearts beat as one!

John Greenleaf Whittier

LITANY OF THE BLACK PEOPLE

Our flesh that was a battle-ground
Shows now the morning-break;
The ancient deities are downed
For Thy eternal sake.
Now that the past is left behind,
Fling wide Thy garment's hem,
That we stay one with Thee in mind,
O Christ of Bethlehem!

The thorny wreath may ridge our brow,
The spear may mar our side,
And on white wood from a scented bough
We may be crucified;
Yet no assault the old gods make
Upon our agony
Shall swerve our footsteps from the wake
Of Thine, toward Calvary.

And if we hunger now and thirst,
Grant our withholders may,
When heaven's constellations burst

Upon Thy crowning day,
Be fed by us—, and given to see
Thy mercy in our eyes,
When Bethlehem and Calvary
Are merged in Paradise.

Countee Cullen

THE LORD CHRIST CAME TO NOTRE DAME

The Lord Christ came to Notre Dame;
Unseen within the shadows there,
He heard the high resounding psalm,
    The chanted immemorial prayer;
From a far wandering He had come,
The length and breadth of Christendom.
'Twas Christmas Eve; a solemn mirth
    Filled the great fane with music sweet,
Singing the gladness of His birth.
    The snow was falling in the street,
    The world went by with homeless feet.
"Peace and good will . . ." Beneath His hood
The tears stole down—His dreams of good
How little had men understood,
    How often calling on His name,
    Had these old streets run wild with flame,
And yonder river roared with blood!
Slaying each other for His sake,
    Marching for Him with fife and drum,
Building with fagot and with stake
    The gentle-hearted world to come,

With torture a new earth to make,
  And call it Christendom;
With fury to make fury cease,
  Dancing in blood, sweet land of France,
  To teach the nations how to dance,
And out of murder to bring peace;
  Forging new chains to make men free.
  And call it Liberty.

The Lord Christ came to Notre Dame;
From a far wandering He had come,
The length and breadth of Christendom,
And whereso'er His feet had trod,
Men, in the holy name of God,
Warred on each other, crying "Peace",
Warring, they cried, that war should cease.
The Lord Christ bowed His head, and smiles
  Brightened His tears, for in His breast,
From the sea's multitudinous miles
  A dove had lighted and taken rest.
Then fell a hush, and in the place
  Of the Lord Cardinal His face
Shone strangely, the strange face of Love,
  And on His lifted hand the dove.
Stilled was the high-resounding psalm,
And then omnipotently calm,
The Lord Christ spake in Notre Dame:
  "Be they forevermore abhorred
  Who calling upon Christ their Lord
  Shall ever draw again this sword!"
So spake Lord Christ in Notre Dame.
                    Richard Le Gallienne

CHRISTMAS AFTER WAR

Shall misery make mirth,
    Lord of our disbelief?
What gift of joy has earth?
    Bring me your grief.

How shall old fables heal
    Our world of woe and sin?
*When you through fable feel
    The truth within.*

There is no guiding star:
    The heavens are black and blind.
*The magi journeyed far;
    So must mankind.*

What singing angels press
    Bright wings down these wild skies?
*Courage and faithfulness
    And sacrifice.*

Madonna, Child, are we
    Shepherds to seek for them?
*Love! Peace! Let your heart be
    Their Bethlehem.*
                        Katherine Lee Bates

THE CONSECRATION OF THE
COMMON WAY

The hills that had been lone and lean
Were pricking with a tender green,
And flocks were whitening over them
From all the fields of Bethlehem.
The King of Heaven had come our way,
And in a lowly stable lay;
He had descended from the sky
In answer to the world's long cry—
Descended in a lyric burst
Of high archangels, going first
Unto the lowest and the least,
To humble bird and weary beast,
His palace was a wayside shed,
A battered manger was his bed;
An ox and ass with breathings deep
Made warm the chamber of his sleep.
Three sparrows with a friendly sound
Were picking barley from the ground;
An early sunbeam, long and thin,
Slanted across the dark within,
And brightened in its silver fall
A cartwheel leaning to the wall.
An ox-yoke hung upon a hook;
A worn plow with a clumsy crook
Was lying idly by the wheel.
And everywhere there was the feel
Of that sweet peace that labor brings—
The peace that dwells with homely things.

Now have the homely things been made
Sacred, and a glory on them laid.
For He whose shelter was a stall,
The King, was born among them all.
He came to handle saw and plane,
To use and hallow the profane;
Now is the holy not afar
In temples lighted by a star,
But where the loves and labors are.
Now that the King has gone this way,
Great are the things of every day.

Edwin Markham

CHRISTMAS

A boy was born at Bethlehem
That knew the haunts of Galilee,
He wandered on Mount Lebanon,
And learned to love each forest tree.

But I was born at Marlborough,
And love the homely faces there;
And for all other men besides
'Tis little love I have to spare.

I should not mind to die for them,
My own dear downs, my comrades true.
But that great heart of Bethlehem,
He died for men he never knew.

And yet, I think, at Golgotha,
As Jesus' eyes were closed in death,
They saw with love most passionate
The village street at Nazareth.
                              E. Hilton Young

HOW CAN THEY HONOR HIM

How can they honor Him—the humble lad
  Whose feet struck paths of beauty through the
    earth—
With all the drunken revelry, the mad
  Barter of goods that marks His day of birth?
How can they honor Him with flame and din,
  Whose soul was peaceful as a moon-swept sea,
Whose thoughts were somber with the world's great sin
  Even while He trod the hill to Calvary?

I think if Jesus should return and see
  This hollow blasphemy, this day of horror,
The heart that languished in Gethsemane
  Would know again as great and deep a sorrow,
And He who charmed the troubled waves to sleep
With deathless words—would kneel again and weep.
                              Anderson M. Scruggs

OUT OF THE SHADOW

Out of the Shadow of the Night
I come, led by the starshine bright,

With broken heart to bring to Thee
The fruit of Thine Epiphany,
The gift my fellows send by me,
The myrrh to bed Thine agony
I set it here beneath Thy feet,
In token of Death's great defeat;
And hail Thee Conqueror in the strife,
And hail Thee Lord of Light and Life,
  All hail! All hail the Virgin Son!
  All hail! Thou little helpless One!
  All hail! Thou King upon the Tree!
  All hail! The Babe on Mary's knee!
    The Centre of all mystery!

Michael Fairless

HORA CHRISTI

Sweet is the time for joyous folk
  Of gifts and minstrelsy;
Yet I, O lowly-hearted One,
  Crave but Thy company.
On lonesome road, beset with dread,
  My questing lies afar,
I have no light, save in the east
  The gleaming of Thy star.

In cloistered aisles they keep to-day
  Thy feast, O living Lord!
With pomp of banner, pride of song,
  And stately sounding word.

Mute stand the kings of power and place,
  While priests of holy mind
Dispense Thy blessed heritage
  Of peace to all mankind.

I know a spot where budless twigs
  Are bare above the snow,
And where sweet winter-loving birds
  Flit softly to and fro;
There with the sun for altar-fire,
  The earth for kneeling-place,
The gentle air for chorister,
  Will I adore Thy face.

Loud, underneath the great blue sky,
  My heart will paean sing,
The gold and myrrh of meekest love
  Mine only offering.
Bliss of Thy birth shall quicken me;
  And for Thy pain and dole
Tears are but vain, so I will keep
  The silence of the soul.

                              Alice Brown

STAR OF MY HEART

Star of my heart, I follow from afar.
Sweet Love on high, lead on where shepherds are,
Where Time is not, and only dreamers are.
Star from of old, the Magi-Kings are dead

And a foolish Saxon seeks the manger-bed.
O lead me to Jehovah's child
Across this dreamland lone and wild.
Thus I will speak this prayer unsaid,
And kiss his little haloed head—
"My star and I, we love thee, little child."

Except the Christ be born again tonight
In dreams of all men, saints and sons of shame,
The world will never see his kingdom bright.
Star of all hearts, lead onward thro' the night
Past death-black deserts, doubts without a name,
Past hills of pain and mountains of new sin
To that far sky where mystic births begin,
Where dreaming ears the angel-song shall win.
Our Christmas shall be rare at dawning there,
And each shall find his brother fair
Like a little child within:
All hearts of the earth shall find new birth
And wake, no more to sin.

Vachel Lindsay

THE CHRISTMAS TREE

If Christ could ever be born again,
   Who would His Mother be?
"I," said Sorrow; and "I," said Pain;
   And "I," said Poverty.

But how, were Christ so made again,
   Could one be born of Three?
"Are not the griefs of earth a strain
   Of the Blessed Trinity?"

And who, on His birth-night, again
   His worshipers would be?
"Love," said Sorrow; and "Pity," said Pain;
   And "Peace," said Poverty.

And who the seers, from what strange lands,
   Would come to look at Him?
"The simple and wise, with serving hands,
   And little ones light of limb."

And what would the kings of earth do then?
   "Put simple and wise to flight;
While loud in the darkened homes of men
   The little ones cried for light."

What use, what use, if once again
   The world rejects the Sign?
"Christ will still be a Lover of men,
   And His heart may be yours and mine.

"For this is the Tree whose blessed yield
   Bears seed in darkest ground;
And a wound by those bright leaves is healed
   Wherever a wound is found."

                      Edward Shillito

Index of Titles

Index of Titles 215

PAGE

Christmas Wish, A. *Celia Thaxter* 195
Come Bring With a Noise. *Robert Herrick* . . 133
Consecration of the Common Way, The. *Edwin Markham* 205
Country Carol, A. *Margaret Widdemer* . . . 102
Courtesy. *Hilaire Belloc* 188
Creche, The. *Carol Ryrie Brink* 157

Deathless Tale, The. *Charles Hanson Towne* . 197

First Best Christmas Night, The. *Margaret Deland* 66
First Christmas, The. *Emilie Poulsson* 146
First Christmas Night of All. *Nancy Byrd Turner* 94
First Nowell, The. *Old Song* 44
From Far Away. *William Morris* 60

Gates and Doors. *Joyce Kilmer* 25
God Rest Ye, Merry Gentlemen. *Dinah Maria Mulock Craik* 5
Golden Carol of Melchior, Balthazar and Gaspar, the Three Kings, The. *Old English* . . . 8
Good King Wenceslas. *Translated from the Latin by J. M. Neale* 187
Gracious Saviour Born of Mary. *Edmund Hamilton Sears, 2nd* 190

Hark! the Herald Angels Sing. *Charles Wesley* 40
Haughty Aspen, The. *Nora Archibald Smith* . . 119
Here We Come A-Whistling. *Old Carol* . . . 131
His Birthday. *May Riley Smith* 96

Index of Authors

220

PAGE

PAGE

Index of First Lines

PAGE

Index of First Lines

233

PAGE